God / Terror

God / Terror
Ethics and Aesthetics in Contexts of Conflict and Reconciliation

Volker Küster

SHEFFIELD UK   BRISTOL CT

Published by Equinox Publishing Ltd.

UK   Office 415, The Workstation, 15 Paternoster Row, Sheffield, South Yorkshire S1 2BX
USA ISD, 70 Enterprise Drive, Bristol, CT 06010

www.equinoxpub.com

Previously published in German as *Gott – Terror: Ein Diptychon* by Kohlhammer 2019. This first English edition published by Equinox Publishing Ltd 2021.

© Volker Küster 2021

All rights reserved. No part of this publication may be reproduced or transmitted in any form or by any means, electronic or mechanical, including photocopying, recording or any information storage or retrieval system, without prior permission in writing from the publishers.

British Library Cataloguing-in-Publication Data

A catalogue record for this book is available from the British Library.

ISBN-13 978 1 80050 092 1 (hardback)
         978 1 80050 093 8 (paperback)
         978 1 80050 094 5 (ePDF)
         978 1 80050 123 2 (ePub)

Library of Congress Cataloging-in-Publication Data

Names: Küster, Volker, 1962- author.
Title: God/terror : ethics and aesthetics in contexts of conflict and reconciliation / Volker Küster.
Other titles: Gott--Terror. English.
Description: Sheffield, South Yorkshire ; Bristol, CT : Equinox Publishing Ltd, 2021. | "Previously published in German as Gott – Terror: Ein Diptychon by Kohlhammer 2019." | Includes bibliographical references and index. | Summary: "God/Terror addresses the quest for God in the context of oppression, violence and terror from an aesthetic perspective. It looks at how artists and writers approach the relationship between God and Terror. As in a medieval diptych, the theme is mirroring god talk in memory of 9/11 and in the context of political conflicts in Germany, South Korea and South Africa"-- Provided by publisher.
Identifiers: LCCN 2021011329 (print) | LCCN 2021011330 (ebook) | ISBN 9781800500921 (hardback) | ISBN 9781800500938 (paperback) | ISBN 9781800500945 (pdf) | ISBN 9781800501232 (epub)
Subjects: LCSH: Terrorism--Religious aspects. | Political violence--Religious aspects. | Art and religion. | September 11 Terrorist Attacks, 2001.
Classification: LCC BL65.T47 K8713 2021 (print) | LCC BL65.T47 (ebook) | DDC 201/.863325--dc23
LC record available at https://lccn.loc.gov/2021011329
LC ebook record available at https://lccn.loc.gov/2021011330

Typeset by Sparks – www.sparkspublishing.com

Contents

List of Illustrations	vii
Prologue	1
I Terror, War and Violence: God Talk in Memory of September 11, 2001	**5**
1 The power of images	6
2 *Apocalypse now* – Does 9/11 mark an epochal boundary?	22
3 Conflicting images of God	24
II Guilt, Reconciliation and Grace: God Talk in the Context of Political Conflicts in Germany, South Korea and South Africa	**31**
1 The powerlessness of images	33
2 Beyond Apocalypse – Dealing with guilt in societal transformation processes	73
3 In conflict with God	80
Epilogue	85
Bibliography	87
Index	95

List of Illustrations

I am grateful to the artists, galleries and museums who have granted me the rights to publish the images free of charge. In two cases, however, in spite of all efforts I was not able to get in touch with the artists. They can contact the publisher for a complimentary copy of the book. For those who requested particular mentioning of size etc. see below. For the others I refer to the respective catalogues in the text, where the works are discussed.

Gerhard Richter in detail:
- Uncle Rudi [*Onkel Rudi*] (85), 1965, oil on canvas, 87 × 50 cm
- Aunt Marianne [*Tante Marianne*] (87), 1965, oil on canvas, 100 × 115 cm
- Mr. Heyde [*Herr Heyde*] (100), 1965, oil on canvas, 55 × 65 cm
- Hanged [*Erhängte*] (668), 1988, oil on canvas, 200 × 140 cm
- Dead [*Tote*] (667–1), 1988, oil on canvas, 62 × 67 cm
- Man Shot Down [*Erschossener 1*] (669–1), 1988, oil on canvas, 100 × 140 cm
- Funeral [*Beerdigung*] (673), 1988, oil on canvas, 200 × 320 cm
- September (891–5), 2005, oil on canvas, 52 × 72 cm

Alfredo Jaar:
- *Lament of the Images*, 2002. Three illuminated texts, light screen, text by David Levi Strauss. Overall dimensions variable. Courtesy Galerie Lelong & Co., New York; Louisiana Museum of Modern Art, Humlebæk; Museum of Modern Art, New York; and the artist, New York.

The photographs of the 9/11 Memorial and Museum (by Paul Sableman) are taken from commons.wikimedia.org.

Prologue

In late modernity, theology has to perform an *aesthetic turn* if it wants to break out of its current isolation. This hypothesis implies that theologians must not limit themselves to biblical texts and Christian tradition as a frame of reference but also should search for traces of God's presence in culture and religion. Along with interdisciplinarity and methodological diversity new literary genres have to be explored theologically. Essay, critique or meditation complement the systematic theological tract.

Aesthetics is understood here as a theory of the perception of sensual manifestations.[1] For me, this implies the thesis that we perceive – for example, the horror orchestrated by the media – in a structurally similar way to the beauty.[2] The classical definition of aesthetics as the theory of the perception of beauty has become shaky. This is the result of the discovery of the artist as individual and the autonomy of the work of art, as well as the indifference and lack of norms that is typical of late modernity as it appears exemplarily in the ambivalence of the mass media. In contemporary art, moreover, the assumption that art is an expression of beauty and therefore of the good is deconstructed. The dialectic between aesthetics and ethics[3] that was originally regarded as constitutive has to be reconstructed case by case today.[4]

In the visual arts and in literature Christian subjects have receded into the background with the rise of modernity. Contemporary artists rarely design sacred spaces. The relationship between the arts and the churches is a difficult one, regarded from either side. At the same time both have in common that they interpret human life and allow experiences of transcendence. Whether human beings succeed in disclosing this transcendent dimension of

---

[1] Cf. Martin Seel, *Ästhetik des Erscheinens*, Frankfurt a.M. 2003 [Engl. 2004].

[2] Cf. Susan Sontag, *Regarding the Pain of Others*, London etc. 2003, 67f.

[3] Cf. Onno Zijlstra, *Ethiek en Esthetiek zijn Eén. Over Wittgensteins Tractatus 6.421*, Kamper Cahiers 69, Kampen 1990.

[4] Cf. Mary Devereux, Beauty and evil: The case of Leni Riefenstahl's *Triumph of the Will*, in: *Aesthetics and Ethics. Essays at the Intersection*, Jerrold Levinson (ed.), Cambridge 1998, 227–256. https://doi.org/10.1017/CBO9780511663888.009

their life is a criterion both for good worship and for good art, even if secular art critics and artists would likely contest this vehemently.

The *generative themes* of human life – like birth, illness, suffering and death, hatred, violence and horror, as well as happiness, friendship and love – are dealt with by artists and theologians alike.[5] In earlier times western art made use of the abundance of biblical stories to illustrate these themes; and later, mythological, historical and literary topics were added. The themes themselves can be found in modern art as well, and are open to Christian interpretation even in accordance with recent developments in art theory. On the other hand, artists make further use of the repertoire of the Christian tradition. Today, however, they work more with fragments than with full stories.

This volume addresses the God question in the context of terrorism and oppression by the state, and its consequences from an aesthetic perspective. Artists are sensitive to what is going on around them and respond intuitively in their artwork; they function like a seismograph, and their reactions are often in the vanguard of the reflections and theories of society in general. The author sees and reads how visual artists and writers approach the relationship between God and terror. Statements like that of the composer Karlheinz Stockhausen, that September 11, 2001 was "the greatest work of art ever",[6] or that of the coloured South African writer Adam Small, that "Only literature can perform the miracle of reconciliation",[7] give rise to new reflections on the relationship between aesthetics and ethics, art and theology. Like in a diptych, the form chosen for the structure of this book, I vary these generative themes in two panels, or chapters, illustrating God talk in memory of 9/11 and in the context of political conflicts in Germany, South Korea and South Africa.

In spite of the prohibition of images in monotheistic religions, God talk is figurative speech. Behind the present *jihad* or "war against evil" (viz. "terror"), a conflict of influential images of God is concealed. The first chapter contrasts works of art that address violence and terror of 9/11 or, in the Muslim world, with the images of 9/11 itself. Alongside the Chilean born Alfredo Jaar and the German of Jewish descent Rebekka Horn, two artists

---

[5] This terminology I owe to the Brazilian educationalist Paulo Freire. The "generative themes" can be derived from their relevance for a community in a particular context, or are fundamental for the identity of a faith community. Cf. Volker Küster, *The Many Faces of Jesus Christ. Intercultural Christology*, Maryknoll, NY 2001, 33–35.

[6] See below (p.13).

[7] See below (p.31).

with Arab Muslim migratory background – Walid Raad and Shirin Neshat – are introduced. In the world of literature, Susan Sontag, Toni Morrison and Arundhati Roy have their say. From this comparative approach three ethical criteria emerge: *vision*, *distance* and *unscathedness*, which also apply to the conflicting images of God. 9/11 does not mark the beginning of a new era, but has become the symbol of the repercussions of globalization, like the collapse of the bipolar world order, the extension of neo-liberal consumer capitalism and the compression of the world through the new communication technologies.[8]

The second chapter exposes the reader to the vulnerability of paintings and novels that deal with the consequences of terrorism by individuals and the state. The Baader-Meinhof cycle of Gerhard Richter is put into dialog with the wood-prints of the South Korean artist Hong Song-Dam that deal with the Kwangju massacre.[9] The novels of Uwe Timm and Hwang Sok-Yong are read *contrapuntally*.[10] These German-Korean passions are confronted with works of the South African artists Sue Williamson and Paul Stopforth that address the murder of Steve Biko. In literature, the magnum opus of Antjie Krog, *Country of my Skull*, gets a forum.

The first chapter concludes that the apocalypse did not take place. Yet how do we deal with guilt in societal processes of transformation? Five themes that regularly reoccur can be identified: resistance against forgetting, the wish to understand what has happened, the expectation that the perpetrators show repentance, the question of whether amnesty or mercy should be granted and the necessity of material reparation. Put in theological language this can lead into a conflict with God. The victims bring their lament before God. They even charge God. How can God allow their suffering? At the same time, especially, the victims show an unbelievable readiness for forgiveness. They

---

[8] Cf. Robert J. Schreiter, *The New Catholicity. Theology between the Global and the Local*, Maryknoll, NY 1997.

[9] The Baader-Meinhof Group named after two of its leading members was a leftist terror organization that declared war against the democratic state of former Western Germany. See below (pp.44–56). In 1980 the army caused a massacre among their own civilian countrymen in the provincial capital Kwangju, that became a symbol of the state terrorism of the South Korean military dictatorship. See below (pp.43–57). For the different forms of terror that become visible here cf. Rudolf Walther, Terror und Terrorismus. Eine begriffs- und sozialgeschichtliche Skizze, in: Wolfgang Kraushaar (ed.), *Die RAF und der linke Terrorismus*, Vol. 1, Hamburg 2006, 64–77.

[10] Cf. R.S. Sugirtharajah, *Postcolonial Reconfigurations. An Alternative Way of Reading the Bible and Doing Theology*, St. Louis 2003, 16 and 170 referring to Edward W. Said, *Culture and Imperialism*, London 1993.

imitate in a certain sense the unconditional grace of God. The perpetrators are disturbed in their relationship with God and rely on the grace of God and the willingness of the victims to reconcile. Already the end of the first chapter points to the justice and compassion of God, in which the victims may feel safe and secure against all ambiguity of human images of God.

I   Terror, War and Violence
God Talk in Memory of September 11, 2001

The following reflections are an attempt to approach the events of September 11, 2001, from aesthetic and theological points of view.[1] This project has been triggered not least because of the provocative dictum by Karl Heinz Stockhausen that 9/11 was "the greatest work of art ever".[2] By confronting art works that grapple with terror and violence in the Arab world with the images of 9/11, ethical criteria are developed that allow an answer to Stockhausen's assertion. For this reconstruction of the relationship between ethics and aesthetics I variegate the classical hermeneutical positions in the relationship of artist, work of art and beholder. The evolving criteria of *vision*, *distance* and *unscathedness* not only refute Stockhausen, but can also help to debunk false images of God.

The power of the images that were unleashed by the terrorists of 9/11 is grounded in a conflict of images of God that drive the combatants either into this *jihad* or the "war against evil or terror" respectively. How can the three criteria developed here be applied in this context? The aesthetic approach to God talk in memory of 9/11 evolves in three stages: in view of the events themselves (1 The power of images), their reception (2 *Apocalypse now* – Does 9/11 mark an epochal boundary?), and a theological reflection (3 Conflicting images of God).

---

[1] Cf. *Kunst nach Ground Zero*, Heinz Peter Schwerfel (ed.), Köln 2002. Earlier versions of this chapter have been published in: *Exchange*, 36, 2007, 231–245; *Evangelische Theologie* 67, 2007, 291–302; *Tijdschrift voor Theologie* 46, 2006, 321–332 as well as in Albert van der Schoot (ed.), *Kunst als morele vrijplaats*, Arnhem 2008, 101–108.

[2] See below (p.13).

1 The power of images

What do we actually remember of the events of 9/11? Or, to put it another way, what has been imprinted in the cultural memory? We might recall the images of the plane gouging its way into the South tower. We might remember the shining colossus, made of glass, steel and concrete, burning and collapsing.[3] We may recollect the images of desperate people jumping to their deaths because their route to survival has been cut off. Or we may call to mind the images of people struck with dismay, restlessly searching the moonscape of Ground Zero. Some of us might remember the images of the Pentagon's destroyed front or the bits and pieces of a plane spread around a field somewhere in Pennsylvania.

The images of the badly damaged Pentagon quickly vanished from the newscast. The fact that the American empire was struck at its most vulnerable spot – i.e. at the headquarters of its military power – did not chime with the threatening gestures in the build up to the war against terrorism.[4] The silent testimonies of several courageous passengers aboard the fourth plane, the debris on the field in Pennsylvania, was eclipsed by the staging of the apocalypse in New York. Yet these images could have reduced the monstrosity of the terrorists to a standard measure. They were defeatable without giant war machinery being activated.

The flow of images coming from the media is obviously steered.[5] Whereas CNN turned the Second Gulf War (1990/91)[6] into a media spectacle, the "war against terrorism" in Afghanistan was a hidden war from its very beginning. In Europe, images of destroyed settlements and dying civilians would have quickly made the public question the alliance against terrorism.

---

[3] In the meantime, a generation has already grown up who did not see these events as they unfolded.

[4] For the empire debate cf. Michael Hardt and Antonio Negri, *Empire*, Cambridge 2000; Kwok Pui-Lan et al. (eds.), *Empire and the Christian Tradition. New Readings of Classical Theologians*, Minneapolis 2007, and the Accra Confession of the 24th Assembly of the World Alliance of Reformed Churches in 2004.

[5] Cf. *Attack. Kunst und Krieg in den Zeiten der Medien*, Katalog zur Ausstellung der Kunsthalle Wien May 23rd–September 21st, 2003, Gabriele Mackert et al. (eds.), Vienna 2003.

[6] The naming, counting and dating of these wars varies. I follow the enumeration that counts the Iran–Iraq war (1980–1988) as the First Gulf War, followed by the conflict around the Iraqi invasion of Kuwait as the Second Gulf War (1990/91) and the American invasion of Iraq as the Third Gulf War (2003 and beyond).

Alfredo Jaar (b. 1956) – who was born in Chile and currently lives in New York – worked with this theme in his installation *Lament of the Images*, which he composed for the occasion of *Documenta 11* in Kassel, Germany (from June 8 till September 15, 2002). Within a first room, with dark walls, a triptych of writing tablets is starkly illuminated. The first tablet refers to Nelson Mandela's release from prison (1990). He squints into the light and cannot shed any tears, for his eyes are permanently damaged by the glaring light inside the limestone pits on Robben Island. The subject of the second tablet is Bill Gates' Microsoft's monopolization of copyrights of images. The third tablet discusses the Pentagon purchasing the exclusive copyrights on picture material in the run-up to the war in Afghanistan. Passing through a dark corridor the visitors reach a second room, which is dazzlingly lit (Figure 1). A side door enables escape.[7]

During the Third Gulf War (since 2003) the military tried to direct the way the media reported the news by working with so-called "embedded journalists". This strategy was later thwarted by comrades displaying pictures of torture practices in Abu Graib on the Internet. With these blurred amateur snapshots, the United States' claim of bringing democracy and human rights to the peoples in the Near East had irreversibly been discredited.

The terrorist attacks of 9/11 also complied with a cunning direction that demanded years of preparation. According to plan, the four hijacked planes would crash into symbols of the economic, political and military power of the US. The intervals between the collisions with both towers would guarantee the presence of the media. The terrorists sovereignly controlled modern means of mass transport and mass communication. At the same time, however, in a seemingly archaic manner, they were prepared to sacrifice their own lives.

Osama Bin Laden, the *spiritus rector* of the attacks of 9/11, is spurred on by a habitus of resentment.

> Behold America, struck by God at its most vulnerable spot. Its highest buildings are ruined. Thanks be to God. Behold America, filled with fear from the north to the south, from the west to the east. Thanks be to God. What America experiences right now, is nothing compared to what we have been experiencing for years. Our community has suffered this humiliation and this degradation for

---

[7] Cf. *Documenta 11_Plattform 5: Austellungsorte*, Ostfildern-Ruit 2002, 56f.

8   *God / Terror*

Figure 1   Alfredo Jaar, *Lament of the Images*

over 80 years. Its sons were killed. Its blood was shed. Its sanctuaries were attacked. And no one hears it. No one notices. When God blessed one of the groups of Islam, spearheads of Islam, they destroyed America. I pray to God, that he will hear them and bless them. [...] These events have divided the world into two camps: the camp of the believers and that of the unbelievers, may God keep you far away from them. Every Muslim must have the urge to help his religion gain the victory. The storm of faith has come. The storm of change has come, to eradicate the oppression of Mohammed's island, peace be with him.⁸

The relationships between the Islamic countries and the West are traumatized by one-and-a-half centuries of merciless colonization. In this respect, the foundation of the state of Israel and its continuous support by the US and its Western allies are interpreted as a continuation of colonialism by different means.⁹ In Bin Laden's view Americans have besmirched the land of his home country Saudi Arabia, in which the holy places of Islam are located.¹⁰ Against this background, he develops a simplistically woven fundamentalist theology of liberation that perverts Islam to a totalitarian ideology. His God is a "God of Terror" who blesses the "spearheads of Islam" in their struggle for the liberation of his holy places.

Until now the fundamentalist movements in the Arab world could count on the support of an estimated maximum of 20–25% of the population.¹¹ In the end, the poor and uneducated people – often oppressed by its own leaders – belong to the losing side of globalization. Fundamentalist aid organizations are often the only ones to offer help. The dropping of food parcels by the US during the bombing of Afghanistan made a mockery of people's dignity. Considering all this, one wonders why not more people succumbed to the whisperings of Bin Laden.

Susan Sontag (1933–2004)¹² was one of the first and most prominent voices that linked the terrorist attacks on the US to their foreign policy. Simultaneously, she certified the courage of the terrorists in their willingness to sacrifice their own lives. By contrast, Sontag labels the military retaliatory air raids as cowardice. She defines courage as "the only

---

[8] Osama Bin Laden quoted by Gottfried Küenzlen, Nach dem 11. September: Fundamentalismus – Phantom oder Phänomen?, in: Hubertus Lutterbach and Jürgen Manemann (eds.), *Religion und Terror. Stimmen zum 11. September aus Christentum, Islam und Judentum*, Münster 2002, 78–93, 80, translations from German sources mine.

[9] Cf. Ian Buruma and Avishai Margalit, *Occidentalism. A Short History of Anti-Westernism*, London 2004.

[10] Ironically the Bin Laden family, which is in the construction business, was involved in building the very American Air bases under question.

[11] Cf. Harald Müller, *Das Zusammenleben der Kulturen. Ein Gegenentwurf zu Huntington*, Frankfurt a.M. 1998, 152.

[12] Cf. Susan Sontag, Feige waren die Mörder nicht, in: *Dienstag 11. September 2001*, Reinbek bei Hamburg 2001, 33–35 [*New Yorker* 24.09.2001]; id., Der Irrtum der Ausnahme, in: *Der Schock des 11. September und das Geheimnis des Anderen. Eine Dokumentation*, Berlin 2002, 40–42.

morally neutral virtue"[13]. A perversion of thought becomes apparent here. The Abrahamic religions – Judaism, Christianity and Islam – need to counter this cynicism with a web of norms and values, which – by means of their assimilative capacity – expose the acts of Bin Laden and his Al Qaida troops for what they are: acts of evil. Courage was rather shown by the passengers of the fourth airplane. When they were informed about the events in New York through their cell phones, they decided to stand up against the terrorists, instead of being led unresisting to slaughter.

While the Islamic mob was burning images of the American president and American flags on the streets, images of Bin Laden were carried around like icons.[14] Reciprocally, in the West, Bin Laden had become the icon of evil. He really was a pop star carrying the odor of destruction. In turn, Indian writer and activist Arundhati Roy (b. 1961) has called American president George W. Bush Bin Laden's twin brother, on the grounds of similar thought patterns.[15] When German anchorman Ulrich Wickert picked up this thought in a magazine article,[16] he had to apologize on television.

In the age of mass media, the borderlines between reality and fiction, art and commerce, noticeably blur. Images and symbols set the discourse. The Third Gulf War becomes an interactive computer game, with Osama Bin Laden and the terrorists of 9/11 as the "wanted" bandits and American president George W. Bush as sheriff. In the 21st century the myth of the Wild West is newly cast. Yet viewing the images only from the surface is misleading. The unscrupulous Islamic fundamentalists are sons of the Arabic middle and upper class, educated by the West. By contrast, Palestinian suicide bombers are predominantly recruited from the lower class. Before Osama Bin Laden and his Al Qaida network turned into deadly enemies, they were allies of the US in the struggle against what used to be the evil power then: Soviet communism.[17] After this opponent was gone, Harvard professor and governmental advisor

---

[13] Sontag, Feige waren die Mörder nicht, 34.

[14] Again, the meaning of the images of Ho Chi Minh and those of Che Guevara for the protest generation of 1968 are also structurally similar.

[15] Cf. *Frankfurter Allgemeine Zeitung* of September 28th, 2001; and also, the interview with Roy in *Die Zeit* of 15 November, 2001.

[16] In magazine *Max*. Cf. *Spiegel online* 3.10.2001.

[17] For the entanglement of the American ruling elite with the House of Saud and the Bin Laden family cf. the controversial documentary *Fahrenheit 9/11* (2004) by Michael Moore.

Samuel Huntington rewrote the scenario.[18] According to him, the vacuum of the Cold War would be filled by the clash of civilizations. As reality TV, 9/11 got ahead of its Hollywood version.[19] Subsequently, some action film premieres were cancelled,[20] but at the same time Hollywood specialists on these kinds of production were assembled to play through the scenarios of possible future attacks in order to enhance terror prevention.

The dead of 9/11 remain notably unreal, like the extras in Hollywood's catastrophe films. Toni Morrison (1931–2019) tried to prevent this by directly speaking to the dead.[21] Thus the victims regain their identities as members of over 60 different countries and of various religions, including hundreds of Muslims.[22] A similar strategy is implied in Johann Baptist Metz's claim that all God talk should be sensitive to theodicy. In the *memoria passionis* the victims are commemorated.[23]

A similar direction of thought is represented by the installation *Book of Ashes* (2002), in which Rebekka Horn (b. 1944), a Jewish artist living in Berlin and Paris, grapples with 9/11 (Figure 2). A mirror fixed to a low, right-angled rostrum and covered with ashes symbolizes the book. Suspended from the ceiling, a mechanically driven golden needle writes imaginary autographs into the ashes, at specific intervals. In the left corner of the room a cello is placed on a stand. Its bow, which is also mechanically driven, produces monotonous sounds at regular interludes.

In Jewish tradition the names of the dead are kept in a memorial book. According to Talmud scholars the word is alive, when it is spoken. What is written lives only during the moment of writing.

---

[18] Cf. Samuel P. Huntington, *Clash of Civilisations and the Remaking of World Order*, New York 1996 and the critique by Harald Müller, *Das Zusammenleben der Kulturen*.

[19] Cf. Charles Martig, Widerstand gegen den Bilderkrieg, in: *Zeitzeichen* 2, 11/2001, 52–54.

[20] E.g. the release of the Arnold Schwarzenegger film *Collateral Damage* was planned for October 5, 2001. The revised version that finally got into the cinemas on February 8, 2002 was shortened with some scenes cut that were too reminiscent of 9/11.

[21] Cf. Toni Morrison, Die Toten des 11. September, in: *Dienstag 11. September*, 11f. [*Vanity Fair* 13.09.2001].

[22] Stefan Aust and Cordt Schnibben also personify victims and assassins in their *11. September. Geschichte eines Terrorangriffs*, Stuttgart etc. 2002².

[23] Johann Baptist Metz, *Memoria Passionis. Ein provozierendes Gedächtnis in pluralistischer Gesellschaft*, Freiburg etc. 2006. See below (p.73).

Figure 2   Rebekka Horn, *Book of Ashes*

And yet precisely as they are uttered, these words are kept from oblivion.[24]

Only the impressive "special effects" seem to be engraved in the cultural memory though: the planes crashing into the towers of the World Trade Center and making them collapse.[25]

Paul Virilio[26] and Indian Christian artist and lay theologian Joti Sahi[27] have both independently interpreted the terrorist attack of 9/11 as iconoclasm. The terrorists behaved like iconoclasts destroying symbols of the

---

[24] Rebecca Horn, *Bodylandscapes. Zeichnungen, Skulpturen, Installationen 1964–2004*, German guide to the exhibition in the art collection of Nordrhein-Westfalen from October 2, 2004 to January 1, 2005. Cf. also the catalogue under the same title.

[25] This is different for those directly involved, survivors, family members, eyewitnesses and New York residents, who live with the images of the ones they lost.

[26] Cf. Paul Virilio, Vom Terror zur Apokalypse, in: *Der Schock des 11. September*, 44–53.

[27] Cf. Joti Sahi, Terrorism and the clash of Civilisations on http://www.asianchristianart.org/news/article6.htm on 3.09.2006.

economic, political and military power of the US. Composer Karlheinz Stockhausen (1928–2007), however, saw this barbarism as an artistic act.

> What happened there is – you all have to reorder your brains now – the greatest piece of art ever. Minds accomplishing something in an act we could never dream of achieving in music, people practicing like crazy for ten years, totally fanatical for one concert, and then they die. That is the greatest piece of art there is within the entire cosmos [...] I could not do that. Compared to that we – as composers – are nothing.[28]

Just as Susan Sontag tried to detach the virtue "courage" from morality, Stockhausen denied every connection between aesthetics and ethics. 9/11 obviously has an aesthetic dimension to it, but it is still a production of evil. The assassins have shown the vulnerability of the American empire on its own territory and, in the process, they have also demonstrated what a few determined people are capable of. The results were fear and trembling in the West and unconcealed jubilation in certain slum areas of the Arab world. The terrorists succeeded in destroying a symbol of the American way of life, and simultaneously created a symbol of evil.

Growing Muslim fundamentalism and terrorism have also challenged artists of Arab descent to speak up. Lebanese born artist Walid Raad (1967), exiled in New York, has formed the Atlas Group (1989–2004). This imaginary foundation was set up to document the contemporary history of Lebanon in a fictitious archive, especially the long years of the Lebanese civil war (1975–1991).[29] Even in the documentary material itself, reality and fiction are indissolubly interwoven. A series of collages entitled *Notebook Volume 38. Already been in a Lake of Fire* makes accessible 17 out of an alleged total of 145 pages from the notebook. Every one of the numbered pages shows pictures of cars, which brand, model and color match one of the cars that were blown to pieces by a car bomb (Figure 3). A covering note in Arab names "date, time and size of the explosion".[30] Only the engine block remains fully intact after such an

---

[28] Quoted from *Zeitzeichen* 2, 11/2001, 59.

[29] Cf. The Atlas Group Archive, www.theatlasgroup1989.org on 18.09.2020. A large part of this oeuvre could be seen at Documenta 11 in Kassel from 8 June to 15 September, 2002. Cf. *Documenta11_Plattform5: Ausstellung, Kurzführer*, Ostfildern-Ruit 2002, 26f.; *Documenta11_Plattform5: Ausstellung, Katalog*, Ostfildern-Ruit 2002, 180–183; *Documenta11_Plattform5: Ausstellungsorte*, Ostfildern-Ruit 2002, 108f.

[30] Cf. *Documenta11_Plattform5: Ausstellung, Katalog*, 182.

14   God / Terror

Figure 3   Walid Raad, *Notebook Volume 38. Already been in a Lake of Fire*

explosion. Thus, the press photographers competed with each other in first finding and then photographing the block, which was often flung hundreds of meters away from the incident. In another series, entitled *My Neck is Thinner Than a Hair: Engines* (Figure 4), Raad assembled 100 of such photographs from real archives.[31]

---

[31] The title could be an allusion to a formulation in Sura 50,16, that Allah is closer to men "than the carotid".

Terror, War and Violence 15

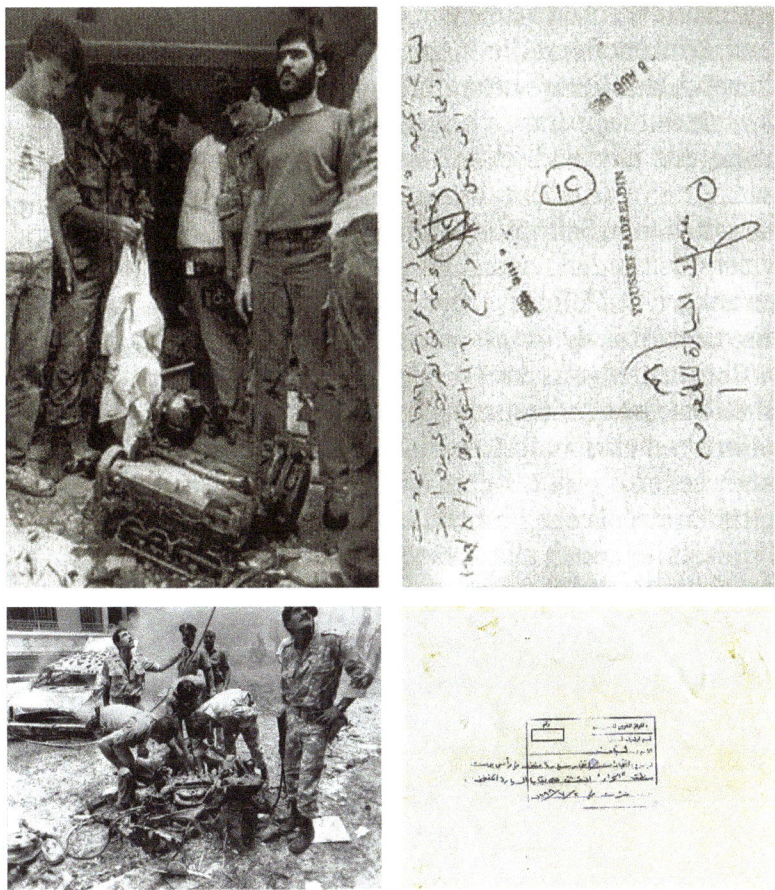

Figure 4   Walid Raad, *My Neck is Thinner Than a Hair: Engines*

Shirin Neshat (b. 1957) is an exile from Iran, who now lives in New York as well. For her early series of photographs called *Women of Allah* (1993–1997), she was inspired by the role of women in the war between Iraq and Iran (First Gulf War, 1980–88).

In this series, I took on the role of those women who fought in the revolution. These women were so committed to their religion that they were able to sacrifice their freedom and their life to promote something larger than themselves. Having lived in the West and focused on my individual interests, I was fascinated by that opposition and what it represented in its pure form.[32]

The black-and-white pictures show women in *chadors*. The artist covered those parts of the body that were unconcealed, such as hands, feet and parts of the face, with handwritten, classical Persian poems in Farsi calligraphy, but also with texts from Islamic fundamentalists and Iranian feminists. In contrast to this, barrels of guns and pistols are pointed at the observer (Figure 5).

In their works, Raad and Neshat approach violence in an aesthetic way. Are they thereby guilty of, say, aesthetic terrorism? In her analysis of Leni Riefenstahl's *Triumph of the Will*, Mary Devereaux offers an artist-oriented perspective, when she introduces the following criterion: "If that vision [the artist's] is flawed, then so is the work of art".[33] At least two criteria should be added here. If one thinks from the perspective of the work of art, one must expect the depiction of evil also to allow for a critical distance from this evil. An observer-oriented approach will claim that the observer's identity might well be questioned, but that he or she may not be mutilated.[34] These criteria are not only to be applied to the aesthetic analysis of works of art, but to all sensorial phenomena.

Both artists obviously create a *distance* from their subjects, Raad by his fictitious archiving and Neshat by the gender perspective that runs through her work.[35] They are both concerned with a critical way of dealing with fundamentalism from an inside perspective. In so doing, they can come under attack from either side. Muslims and Western observers alike feel provoked and questioned in their identities. Nevertheless, they

---

[32] *Shirin Neshat*, Exhibition catalogue ARoS Aarhus Art Museum 2002, 31.

[33] Devereaux, Beauty and Evil, 250.

[34] This might sound absurd but one has to recall the self-mutilation by artists like Rudolf Schwarzkogler (1940–1969) and Günter Brus (b. 1938) from the circle of the Wiener actionists. Cf. Peter Weiermair, Überlegungen zum Thema Blut in der zeitgenössischen Kunst, in: *Blut. Kunst, Macht, Politik, Pathologie*, James M. Bradburne (ed.), München etc. 2001, 205–217. The aforementioned exhibition *Attack. Kunst und Krieg in den Zeiten der Medien* started with the video installation *Barbed Hula* (2000) by Sigalit Landau, that addresses the Palestine conflict. A Hula-ring made of barbed wire is swinging in rhythmic movement around the naked torso of the artist cutting wounds in the skin. In the background the sea breaks against the beach of Tel Aviv. Cf. *Attack*, 110f.

[35] Her latest works shown in a retrospective by the Stedeldijk Museum in Amsterdam (2006) blur the borders between video art and short film and are an expression of an increasingly critical attitude towards Islam.

Terror, War and Violence 17

Figure 5 Shirin Neshat, *Women of Allah*. RC print (photo by Larry Barns) 46¾ × 33⅞ inches. Editon of 10+1 AP. © Shirin Neshat; Courtesy Gladstone Gallery, New York

are not violated. In contrast, the murderous events of 9/11 do not hold up alongside the criteria of *vision*, *distance* and *unscathedness*.

To return to our initial question: what do we actually remember of the events of 9/11? One prominent example relates to the artist Gerhard Richter, who was on his way to the opening of an exhibition of his latest works in the Marian Goodman Gallery in Manhattan, when his flight was

18 *God / Terror*

Figure 6   Gerhard Richter, *September*

redirected to Canada due to the attacks. He finally had to return to Germany without having achieved anything. In 2005, he tackled the resulting barrage of images in his typical manner; but for him in a rather unusual, intimate format of 52×72 cm (Figure 6).

The twin towers are silhouetted, as silver-grey columns against the luminescent light blue of the sky. The method of scraping and blurring the wet paint with a metal spatula – a common feature of his large-scale abstract paintings (for this particular painting Richter used a kitchen knife)[36] – reaches over the whole height of the canvas and defamiliarizes the picture. At the same time, it is reminiscent of the deformation of the collapsing buildings and the devastation of the urban canyons by the rain of ashes. The eye needs time to discover, in the dominating blue and grey tints of the painting, traces of red and orange, which are both remnants of the painting-over technique, and a blurred reminder of the

---

[36] Robert Storr, *September. A History Painting by Gerhard Richter*, London 2009, 47.

fireball, which resulted from the crash of United Airlines Flight 175 into the South tower. With *September* Richter succeeds, in a subtle manner, in deconstructing the images of the mass media burned-in to our retinas.

Another viewpoint has been pursued by the previously unknown architect Michael Arad (b. 1969) and the experienced landscape architect Peter Walker (b. 1932) with their *9/11 memorial* on Ground Zero (Figures 7–9). They inscribe the names of the victims into the topography of terror. The duo confront the overwhelming memory of the images with the memorializing of the names of the victims.

The completion of the memorial site has been a long time coming, and rubbernecks have been kept away from the construction site by hoardings. Today in the *Eatery* – a food court within a luxury Italian supermarket on the first floor of the newly constructed World Trade Center 4 – whoever manages to get hold of one of the in-demand window seats can look out onto a plaza planted with trees, framed by the six newly constructed skyscrapers. The trees, planted in a file, appear from this perspective as a forest from which the entrance hall of the underground 9/11

Figure 7   Michael Arad/Peter Walker, *9/11 memorial*

Figure 8　Michael Arad/Peter Walker, *9/11 memorial*

Museum protrudes. A single pear tree (*survivor tree*) hails from the old plaza in front of the twin towers.

The viewers are, however, also confronted with the northern of the two pools – huge inversive fountains, that fill the footprints of the former twin Towers. In a square, from all four sides, thin walls of water fall into the deep. The water is collected in a basin; in its center it disappears into another square void, the bottom of which cannot be seen from the fringes of the facility above. From the surrounding bronze rim, the names of the victims are cut out, to pluck them from the abyss of the waters of forgetfulness.

The archeology of terror has excavated the foundations of the two towers in the subjacent halls of a gargantuan necropolis. The curiosities of horror – distorted elements of the buildings, rescue vehicles and scattered personal belongings – cannot compete with the atmospheric depression caused by the room itself, in which the matter of the two, collapsed, virtually fused-in buildings has been compacted, immuring the mortal remains of the victims. They are commemorated in a black cube, inside of which the portraits of the dead are displayed in closely spaced

Figure 9 Michael Arad/Peter Walker, *9/11 memorial*

rows. Touchscreens reveal more about individual victims. Private photographs and memories by family and friends give the particular person contour. Viewers can share their inquiries, with a mouse click, with other visitors, who have taken a seat in an inner cube with projection screens. This personalized approach has also been chosen at other points of the exhibition, e.g. when survivors or rescuers have their say. These are powerful elements of the memorial, when the victims are taking center stage alongside the solidarity and pride of the New Yorkers.

In contrast is the intolerable historical misrepresentation within the corridor that describes the rise of Al Qaida. The first act of the drama – Osama Bin Laden's engagement in the Soviet–Afghan war, and the support of the Taliban in the Pakistani–Afghan borderland by the CIA and Pakistani secret service as compliant subsidiaries in the struggle against the then communist arch-enemy the Soviet Union – has simply been omitted.

While the custom of putting a rose into the void letters of the name on the birthday of a victim is an act of individual remembrance, the checkered sea of American flags spread above all names on occasion is a nationalistic misappropriation. The interlocking of nationalism and commerce will always make this site appear in an odd twilight in spite of all good intentions, and sits uncomfortably with the claim by Toni Morrison and Johann Baptist Metz that the dangerous memory of the victims has to be maintained. This dissonance is also apparent in the reference to the façade of the original twin towers, in the architectural design of the cupola above the Westfield World Trade center: a giant underground shopping mall with annex subway station located on the western corner of the plaza. Like a haphazard cenotaph, distorted parts of that façade once surmounted Ground Zero.

2 *Apocalypse now* – Does 9/11 mark an epochal boundary?

"This event has changed the world!" "Nothing will ever be the same!" Among the initial reactions to 9/11, these slogans were most frequent. Apocalypse run rampant.[37] The media were enraptured by images that flickered across the channels in endless chains. Revenge was loudly demanded. Thoughtful voices were filtered out. Whoever dared to question the grounds for the hatred towards the US, which had just been unleashed, was pilloried. Politicians of every persuasion called for security laws to be tightened up. Thus, democracy and its right for freedom of opinion – which the terrorists had allegedly attacked – were hastily sacrificed.

The reactions of the world public, however, remained quite ambivalent. Whereas the Western allies considered the terrorist attack to be an assault upon the liberal democratic order and secured their unreserved solidarity – with British Prime Minister Tony Blair and German Chancellor Gerhard Schröder in the lead[38] – critical voices were raised in Eastern

---

[37] Cf. Jürgen Moltmann, Das Ende als Anfang, in: *Zeitzeichen* 2, 12/2001, 40–43, who sets the Christian expectation for the future against apocalyptic thinking. "For its focus is not the end of life, the end of history or the end of the world, but the beginning of the true life, the kingdom of God and the recreation of all things to their lasting form" (40). A quite different understanding of apocalypticism in the sense of "exposure" – "the exposure of the limitation of the time of the world" as well as "an exposure of the countenance of the victims against the merciless amnesia of the victors" – can be found in Metz, *Memoria*, 137f.

[38] Unlike Blair, Schröder however opted publicly against military counter strikes from the beginning.

Europe and the Global South.³⁹ Russian President Wladimir Putin indeed hastened to join the alliance against terror, as he had problems with Islamists in his own backyard, but he also allowed himself to point out that the Americans were applying double standards as they tried to leave out Saudi Arabia. Arab politicians distanced themselves from the terrorist attacks, but also referred to their roots in America's foreign policy. In the Global South questions concerning the equal value of all human lives were raised, with reference to the hundreds of thousands of victims of poverty and oppression.⁴⁰ The idea that 9/11 marks an epochal boundary is therefore primarily a Western one.

A change of perspective occurs when we pose the question: does 9/11 mark an epochal shift from the point of view of postcolonial criticism and globalization theories? During the spring of 2001, the then New York based Nigerian curator of *Documenta 11* in Kassel, Okwui Enwezor (1963–2019), organized an exhibition of modern African art entitled *The Short Century. Independence and Liberation Movements in Africa, 1945–1994* in Munich.⁴¹ Enwezor connects the beginning of the twentieth century for Africa with the end of World War II. The wave of decolonization that was then set in motion, led to the creation of independent states and cultural renaissances. The African heritage was rediscovered and an African identity was reconstructed. This was the beginning of African modernity. A process that came to a certain end as the first free elections were held in South Africa in 1994.⁴² Enwezor therefore emphasized that, from an African point of view, 9/11 does not affect "our" thinking.⁴³

---

[39] Cf. also the collage of short films *11'09"01 – September 11*, 2002, in which 11 filmmakers (Danis Tanovic, Ken Loach, Sean Penn et al.) from 11 nations offer their view on 9/11 in short films of 11 minutes.

[40] Thus, Tanzanian theologian Laurenti Magesa, on the occasion of a conference in November 2001 in Utrecht. Similarly, Tinyiko Maluleke, Of Collapsible Coffins and Ways of Dying. The Search for a Catholic Contextuality in African Perspective, in: *The Ecumenical Review* 54, 2002, 313–332, 315f. and 318. https://doi.org/10.1111/j.1758-6623.2002.tb00156.x

[41] Okwui Enwezor, *The Short Century. Independence and Liberation Movements in Africa 1945–1994*, München etc. 2001.

[42] Cf. Musa W. Dube, *Postcolonial Feminist Interpretation of the Bible*, St. Louis, Missouri 2000, 3f.

[43] On the occasion of a conference at Hofgeismar Evangelical Academy on November 25th, 2001. Cf. Klaus H. Grabowski, Die Stimmen der Intellektuellen und ihr Echo, in: Felicitas von Aretin and Bernd Wannenmacher (eds.), *Weltlage: Der 11. September, die*

From the perspective of globalization theories, it is the year 1989 that marks an epochal boundary. It is politically characterized by a collapse of the bipolar world order and a crisis of nation states. This is accompanied by the worldwide expansion of neo-liberal capitalism and the compression of the world through new communication technologies.[44] At the same time a *glocalization* of cultures can be observed.[45] Local cultures gain strength in a hybrid, or creolized form. Hence, the myth of cultural authenticity is finally unmasked. Cultures are mixtures of different influences, which nevertheless retain a local distinctness. Globalization creates plural modernities, which perpetuate the old tension between particularity and universality in a new form. This pluralism belies the prophets of the globalized world order, Francis Fukuyama and Samuel Huntington. We have not arrived at the "end of history"[46] nor do we stand at the abyss of a "clash of civilizations"; the apocalypse has failed to materialize.

If 9/11 is not an epochal boundary, then what is it? Early on, German sociologist Ulrich Beck (1944–2015) determined possible repercussions of globalization – i.e. the risks for the world population – such as environmental disasters and also terrorist attacks.[47] For us in the West, 9/11 has become a symbol for these effects of globalization. The images of the collapsing twin towers are therefore printed in our memory as indelible icons of the twenty-first century, which had just begun.

3 Conflicting images of God

From aesthetics and reception aesthetics points of view, the events of 9/11 emerge as an extremely symbolically charged happening. We will turn now towards the religious dimension of this war of images and symbols. What images of God guide the opponents and how can we counteract them theologically?

Politik und die Kulturen, Opladen 2002, 195–208, 207f. In a similar way, Laurenti Magesa expressed himself at the conference in Utrecht referred to earlier.

[44] Cf. Schreiter, *The New Catholicity*.

[45] Cf. Roland Robertson, Glocalization: Time–Space and Homogenity–Heterogenity, in: Scott Lash and Roland Robertson (eds.), *Global Modernities*, London 1995, 25–44.

[46] Francis Fukuyama, *End of History and the Last Man*, New York 1992.

[47] Cf. Ulrich Beck, *Was ist Globalisierung?*, Frankfurt a.M. 1997 [Engl. 1999].

The assassins of 9/11 viewed themselves as warriors of God, as combatants in a *jihad* against "Jews and Crusaders."[48]

> The ruling to kill the Americans and their allies – civilians and military – is an individual duty for every Muslim who can do it in any country in which it is possible to do it, in order to liberate the al-Aqsa Mosque and the holy mosque [Mecca] from their grip, and in order for their armies to move out of all the lands of Islam, defeated and unable to threaten any Muslim. This is in accordance with the words of Almighty Allah, "and fight the pagans all together as they fight you all together," and "fight them until there is no more tumult or oppression, and there prevail justice and faith in Allah."[49]

Thus, the members of both other Abrahamic religions, Judaism and Christianity, are viewed as opponents. The terrorists can link their ideas up with centuries-old stories of conflict. Already the Qur'anic perception of Jews and Christians as "people of the Book" (Sura 3,64 et al.) remains ambivalent. Even though they believe in the same God, they tend to be heretical and try to lead the Muslims astray from the true faith. Later tradition still guarantees them protection within the "House of Islam" as tributaries (*jizyah*).

Further, the conviction that whoever dies as a martyr of Islam will be rewarded with the pleasures of paradise (Sura 4,74; 47,4–6 et al.) is also significant in keeping up the fighting spirit.[50] Since the terrorists were convinced that their deeds were pleasant to God, they accepted taking the lives of innocent people, including women and children, as they took their own. The Qur'an prohibits however the killing of innocent people (Sura 5,31; 6,152; 17,33; 25,68; see also 4,29). With reference to the sayings of the prophet (*hadith*), Islamic tradition also rejects suicide.[51] Reverence for the God-given life is a high virtue in all Abrahamic religions.

---

[48] Cf. *Jihad Against Jews and Crusaders. World Islamic Front Statement*, https://fas.org/irp/world/para/docs/980223-fatwa.htm on 05.08.2020; Stephan Rosiny, Der jihad im Islam, ein kontroverses Rechtsgutachten von 1998 und die Anschläge vom 11. September, in: *Weltlage*, 75–89. https://doi.org/10.1007/978-3-322-95043-7_5

[49] Quotation from *Jihad against Jews and Crusaders*. Bin Laden apparently argues with hackneyed phrases from the Qur'an (Cf. e.g. Sura 9,36).

[50] Navid Kermani, Die Gärten der Märtyrer, in: *Religion und Terror*, 63–75.

[51] Cf. Al-Bukhari 2/23, 445,446 et al.

The crusader rhetoric of American President George W. Bush (b. 1946; in office 2001–2009) touched old traumas of Christian–Muslim relations and triggered outrage in the Arab world. Christian fundamentalism – closely entwined with the then governing Republicans – encourages thinking in terms of a holy war. The strongest argument against this Christian legitimization of violence is the interpretation of Jesus' death on the cross that regards it as God himself walking the path of passion. During the twentieth century, the theology of the cross was actualized by both political theology after Auschwitz and the theologies of liberation in this line of thought. "In the suffering Minjung, the poor and oppressed Korean people, we encounter the suffering Christ," said one of my teachers, Minjung theologian Ahn Byung-Mu (1922–1996).[52] For a long time, this offer of identification gave the poor and oppressed in the Global South new hope. In the course of globalization, however, the gulf between the rich and the poor is getting wider and wider, while the world is no longer paying it great attention. In contrast the theodicean sensibility called for repeatedly by Johann Baptist Metz is meant to preserve the dangerous memory of the martyrdom of the poor and oppressed.[53]

God talk has also received interesting stimulus for renewal by contextual theologies regarding the issues at stake here. Inculturation theologies, which seek their theological foundation in incarnation, God's relatedness to the world in a concrete human being – often with a kenotic accent – has led to a late recognition of cultural difference from the Christian side. How controversial these attempts to inculturation may have been in detail, their consequences for liturgy and church architecture especially in the catholic domain are apparent. Western Christianity, which is exposed to multicultural societies that are characterized by the interaction between the hyperculture of global consumer capitalism and hybrid subcultures has to demonstrate its capability to inculturate itself anew. Meanwhile God, who has already been declared dead in Europe,

---

[52] Cf. Volker Küster, *Theologie im Kontext. Zugleich ein Versuch über die Minjung-Theologie*, Nettetal 1995; id., *Jesus und das Volk im Markusevangelium. Ein Beitrag zum interkulturellen Gespräch in der Exegese*, Neukirchen-Vluyn 1996; id., *A Protestant Theology of Passion. Minjung Theology revisited*, Leiden 2010.

[53] Cf. Metz, *Memoria Passionis*.

has returned in many shapes.[54] In the Christian migrant churches as well as in the mosques of different Muslim communities.

The rediscovery of the relationality of God is also of importance in recent contributions to Trinitarian theology. This is true for God talk in reflexive late modern pluralism in the West[55] as well as in the hybrid modernities of the metropolitan areas in Africa, Asia and Latin America. Jürgen Moltmann and Leonardo Boff, by referring to Karl Rahner, have both equated immanent and economic Trinitarian teaching and exemplified its social dimension.[56] Boff explicitly focuses on the community of the poor and oppressed. For Raimundo Panikkar, on the other hand, Trinitarian teaching in the form of the "cosmotheandric intuition" became a kind of world formula.[57] The discovery of post-Barthian theology, that God is not at the disposal of any religion, and therefore also not a *Christian* God, but the one and only,[58] is controversial intra-Christian as well as inter-religiously. Yet this thought means something quite different from the credo of post-modern relativity "we all believe in the same God". It is the motivating force for an interreligious dialogue about our images of God that understands itself as a common search for truth.

An important aspect of this discourse is the interreligious critique of patriarchal images of God. In critical discussion with second wave Christian feminist theologians, whose intercultural and interreligious bias they clearly emphasize, Jewish, Muslim, Hindu and Buddhist women speak up claiming the religious founding figures and the Holy Scriptures for their ends.[59] It is this intra-religious critique that has the biggest poten-

---

[54] Cf. Friedrich Wilhelm Graf, *Die Wiederkehr der Götter. Religion in der modernen Kultur*, München 2004; id., *Götter global. Wie die Welt zum Supermarkt der Religionen wird*, München 2014.

[55] Cf. Eric Borgman, *Metamorfosen. Over religie en moderne cultuur*, Kampen 2006.

[56] Cf. Jürgen Moltmann, *Trinität und Reich Gottes. Zur Gotteslehre*, München 1980, 176; Leonardo Boff, *Der dreieinige Gott*, Düsseldorf 1987, 244. Immanent trinitarian teaching deals with the inner-trinitarian relationship between God, Son and Holy Spirit, economic Trinitarian teaching with their relationship to the world.

[57] Cf. http://www.raimon-panikkar.org/english/gloss-cosmotheandric.html on 8.11.2020.

[58] Cf. Werner Jeanrond, Thinking about God Today, in: Werner G. Jeanrond and Aasulf Lande (eds.), *The Concept of God in Global Dialogue*, Maryknoll, New York 2005, 89–97.

[59] Cf. the writings of Judith Plaskow, Amina Wadud, Fatima Mernissi and Vandana Shiva; further Phyllis Trible and Letty M. Russel (eds.), *Hagar, Sarah and their Children. Jewish, Christian and Muslim Perspectives*, Louisville, Kentucky 2006.

tial of self-purification of the respective tradition from fundamentalist tendencies. Muslim women can therefore play a central role in the overcoming of the crisis of Islam. With eco-feminism, women have also confronted the destruction of our habitat through the excesses of global neo-liberal capitalism. Christian theologians can refer here to the renaissance of the talk about God the creator in the context of the ecological movements of the 1980s.[60]

The theological irruptions in the second half of the 20th century – liberation theologies, new political theology and feminist theologies, inculturation and dialogue theologies as well as ecological theologies – have grown to global theological flows[61] that counteract reconfessionalization and particularization of Christian theology and churches. They formulated generative themes for God talk in the global risk society: God opts for the poor, is non-gendered, created human kind in their cultural difference and accepts them as such, preserves creation and is present in it and is not available for religious claims to absoluteness of any kind.

In Islamic and Christian fundamentalism, religion becomes ideology and the worship of God becomes idolatry. On the other hand, it cannot be denied, that speech of holy war can be found in the Torah, the Bible and the Qur'an, with JHWH (Yahweh) waging war and the Qur'an praising martyrs. "The dark sides of God" shimmer through the central narratives of the Jewish-Christian-Islamic tradition.[62] God drowned his own creation in the Flood (Gen 6–7; Sura 7,59–64 et al.), he commanded Abraham to sacrifice his son (Gen 22,2; Sura 37,100–107), he allowed his own son to die on the cross (Mark 15 par). Yet, there is also the image of the just and merciful God (Sura 110), who enters into the covenant with Noah (Gen 9), who at the last moment prevents Abraham from sacrificing his son (Gen 22,11–13; Sura 37,100–107), and who overcomes death through resurrection (Mark 16 par).

---

[60] Cf. Jürgen Moltmann, *Gott in der Schöpfung. Ökologische Schöpfungslehre*, München 1987³.

[61] Cf. Schreiter, *The New Catholicity*, 15–21; Volker Küster, Von der lokalen Theologie zur neuen Katholizität. Robert J. Schreiters Suche nach einer Theologie zwischen dem Lokalen und dem Globalen, in: *Evangelische Theologie* 63, 2003, 362–374. https://doi.org/10.14315/evth-2003-0506

[62] Cf. Walter Dietrich and Christian Link, *Die Dunklen Seiten Gottes*, 2 Vols., Neukirchen-Vluyn 1997² and 2000; Horst Hirschler, Wo war Gott am 11. September?, in: *Zeitzeichen* 2, 11/2001, 14–17; Lee Griffith, *The War on Terrorism and the Terror of God*, Grand Rapids 2002.

Within this ambivalence, we must do theology.[63] The three ethical criteria of *vision, distance* and *unscathedness* introduced above prove of value also in the struggle of the concurring images of God.[64] The vision of God who is present in creation counteracts the vision of God of Holy War, who is bringing destruction. All God talk must maintain a distance from, and be aware of, its human limitations as well as the eventual indisposability of God. An instrumentalization of God that leads to the violation of creation discredits itself.

The conflicting images of God are firmly rooted in our tradition. The prohibition of images reminds us to verify whether our images of God are in harmony with the narratives that nourish them.[65] Every illustration is also a fixation of meaning. The storytelling and interpreting Jewish, Christian and Islamic communities share a great treasure of narratives with each other. In spite of the differences, all three Abrahamic religions share in the promises of the same God.[66] Within interreligious dialogue, this kinship can help judge "texts of terror"[67] as well as images and symbols of evil by using narratives on the justice and grace of God, time and again.

---

[63] Cf. Metz, *Memoria Passionis*, 13 and 23f.

[64] See above (p.16f.).

[65] Cf. Christian Link, Das Bilderverbot als Kriterium theologischen Redens von Gott, in: id., *Die Spur des Namens. Wege zur Erkenntnis Gottes und zur Erfahrung der Schöpfung. Theologische Studien*, Neukirchen-Vluyn 1997, 3–35; id., Gott ist ein Fremdling, in: *Zeitzeichen* 3, 6/2002, 26–29.

[66] Cf. Volker Küster, Indebted to Kinship – The Project of an "Abrahamic ecumene" Contested, in: id. and Gé Speelman (eds.), *Islam in the Netherlands. Between Religious Studies and Interreligious Dialogue*, Münster 2010, 163–180.

[67] Cf. Phyllis Trible, *Texts of Terror. Literary-Feminist Readings of Biblical Narratives*, Philadelphia 1984; Dorothea Erbele-Küster, Ungerechte Texte und gerechte Sprache. Überlegungen zur Hermeneutik des Bibelübersetzens, in: *Die Bibel – übersetzt in gerechter Sprache? Grundlagen einer neuen Übersetzung*, Gütersloh 2005, 222–234.

II Guilt, Reconciliation and Grace
God Talk in the Context of Political Conflicts in Germany, South Korea and South Africa

During the interviews for the nomination of the members of the South African Truth and Reconciliation Commission the coloured writer Adam Small (b. 1936),[1] one of the candidates himself, postulated: "Only literature can perform the miracle of reconciliation."[2] He thereby reconstitutes the dialectic between ethics and aesthetics. I tend to rid Small's controversial statement of its exclusivism and at the same time extend it to the artistic production at large. The modified thesis then reads as follows: "Art can anticipate the miracle of reconciliation and serve as a catalyst in societal transformation processes." This thesis is embodied in the living sculpture that the artist duo Elmgreen & Dragset directed for the exhibition *Made in Germany* in the Sprengel Museum Hannover (2007). Close to the entrance inside one of the exhibition halls a young actor dressed in everyday clothes stands on a platform silently handing out little cards to the visitors on which poses the question "Have you come here for forgiveness". Those accepting the card are first of all confronted with themselves. It evokes the question of possible personal guilt. At the same time this declares the exhibition space, and with it the arts, to be a (sacred) space of reconciliation.[3]

The hypothesis formulated above shall be tested in what follows by a close reading and interpretation of the works of painters and writers from Germany, South Korea and South Africa, who are dealing with questions of guilt, reconciliation and mercy in the societal transformation processes of their countries. Because of the particular proximity of the historic experiences of their native countries the two painters Gerhard Richter and

---

[1] Small, who was closely associated with the *Black Consciousness Movement*, is one of the most prolific representatives of the *coloureds* of the South African cape province.

[2] Quoted in Antjie Krog, *Country of my Skull*, London 1999, 26.

[3] Cf. *Made in Germany. Kurzführer / Short Guide*, Hannover 2007, 98.

Hong Song-Dam as well as the writers Uwe Timm and Hwang Sok-Yong are brought into dialog first. This is followed by a comparison with some South African artists.

The aesthetic question is again interwoven with a theological one: to what extend can secular art be interpreted theologically? Or to put it the other way round: how far can theological language elucidate secular circumstances? Christian vocabulary like, for example, forgiveness, reconciliation or grace/mercy has expanded into resolving secular transformation processes.[4] Accordingly, the scenarios of horror (1 The powerlessness of images) are followed by a reflection on how to cope with such traumatic experiences (2 Beyond Apocalypse) that finally leads into a theological meditation (3 In conflict with God).

---

[4] Cf. John W. de Gruchy, *Reconciliation. Restoring Justice*, Minneapolis 2002; Ralf K. Wüstenberg, *The Political Dimension of Reconciliation. A Theological Analysis of Ways of Dealing with Guilt during the Transitions to Democracy in South Africa and Germany*, Grand Rapids and Cambridge 2009.

1 The powerlessness of images

The artists introduced here deal in their works with horrible suffering, which they themselves have often experienced firsthand. They seem to stand powerless against these experiences. From this position of vulnerability, the will to reconciliation arises, even if initially one-sided, with their own violated identity. The initiative to reconciliation lies often enough with the victims and not with the perpetrators.

Germany and Korea, the home countries of the artists discussed first, are connected through their recent historical experiences, in spite of all cultural differences. Germany experienced a fascist regime (1933–45) followed immediately by a communist dictatorship in the east of the divided country (1945–89). In Korea, Japanese colonialism (1905/10–45) was followed in the South by an autocratic phase (1945–60) and a number of military governments (1961–88), interrupted only by a short democratic intermezzo. In 1945, a communist regime established itself in the North.

Indeed, both countries were divided after the end of World War II. Yet while the Germans were perpetrators, the Koreans were victims. Their hopes for freedom and independence after being released from the yoke of Japanese colonialism were distorted by the upcoming east–west conflict. Korea was divided lastingly along the 38th Parallel. From 1950–53 a bloody civil war spread throughout the country. The iron curtain was woven more densely in Korea than in Germany. While the Germans were allowed to have certain contacts across the border, even after the construction of the wall, Koreans were forbidden even to write letters. South Koreans were interested observers of German reunification and learned their lessons for reunification that, in spite of everything, they envisioned for their own country.

Only the historic meeting in 2000 of the two Kims – South Korea's president Kim Dae-Jung (1924–2009; in office 1997–2002) and his North Korean counterpart Kim Young-Il (1941–2011; in office 1994–2009) – resulted in a temporary, precautious opening, which became known as "sunshine politics". However, after repeated periods of governance by the old power elites under Lee Myung-Bak (b. 1941; 2008–2013) and Park Geun-Hye (b. 1952; 2013–2017), the relationship with the North noticeably deteriorated. This was accelerated by the inauguration of North Korean leader Kim Jong-Un (b. 1984; in office since 2001), the third potentate of the Kim Dynasty. While the wounds of the cold war on the Korean peninsula were barely cicatrized, they burst open again in the Putin and Trump eras.

Hong Song-Dam, born in 1955 on the island of Haui and raised in Kwangju, is a real son of the rebellious Cholla province. In his youth he worked as a studio assistant until his talent was discovered, which then enabled him to study fine arts at the Chosun University in Kwangju. His university years were overshadowed by poverty, that forced him to earn money to sustain his living, and by severe tuberculosis from which he suffered. In the sanatorium Hong came in contact with those workers who had become sick through poor working conditions, and social activists who were seeking shelter there from the police and the secret service.[5] The artist became politically conscientized and took part in the 1980 Kwangju uprising. The fact that he survived the bloody suppression of the revolt gave rise to a sense of obligation in his art: "To pay off for my survival I want to portray my time!"[6]

For the regime, Hong's political involvement made him a suspect. In July 1989 the artist was arrested because of an alleged violation of the national security law. He had sent slides of the mural painting, *The history of the national liberation movement of Korea*, which he had painted together with about 200 other artists, to the World Youth festival in Pyongyang, North Korea's capital. The painting that had been destroyed by the South Korean police was reconstructed there in the original format by North Korean artists. Hong was tortured and put into solitary confinement. As a result, Amnesty International adopted him as prisoner of conscience in October 1989.[7] After his release from prison in 1992 he first lived as a freelance artist in Kwangju. Yet in 2000 Hong decided to move to Illsan near the 38th Parallel – both because he wanted to gain some distance from Kwangju and to work for Korean reunification. In spring 2005, after getting married, he resettled in Ansan, an area where many migrant workers live. The artist started to engage in cultural work with them.

Woodcuts were Hong's preferred medium for a long time. He found his subjects in the life of the common people. Apart from the depressing scenes of the Kwangju massacre, he mainly concentrated on events of

---

[5] Cf. *Unerwünschte Bilder. Hong, Sung-Dam. Holz und Linolschnitte aus Südkorea*, ed. by Evangelische Erwachsenenbildung Niedersachsen, Göttingen 1990, 35.

[6] *Malttugi. Texte und Bilder aus der Minjung Kulturbewegung in Südkorea*, Lim Chung-Hee and Andreas Jung (eds.), Heidelberg 1986, 144.

[7] The trial and its further details are documented in: *Unerwünschte Bilder*, 11–29.

everyday life, illustrations of traditional tales, but also religious topics. Hong frequently draws upon traditional Korean stylistics, profiting from having been trained in Buddhist painting (*t'eanghwa* and *tanchong*) and from restoring old Korean cultural assets together with his master.

Gerhard Richter was born 1932 in Dresden. The Nazi dictatorship left its mark on the first thirteen years of his life. Half of this time Germany was at war. The division of the country in 1945 brought a direct transition into a communist system. In 1961, just before the erection of the Berlin wall, Richter ceased his career as rising artist of socialist realism and went West. Having already trained as an artist in the East, Richter enrolled anew at the art academy in Düsseldorf. Under the influence of the West German art scene his style changed and his personal hour zero arrived. The catalogue of his works, kept by the artist himself, does not list his early production. Richter found his own style in a kind of photographic painting. In times when painting was frowned upon, he stuck to it, by recycling traditional genres such as still life, portrait and landscape. Even whilst Richter experimented successfully with abstract painting he always returned to the figurative.

While Hong Song-Dam is a decisive political artist, Gerhard Richter always emphasizes aesthetical questions. Nevertheless, his oeuvre includes, alongside occasional abstract paintings, both the above-mentioned genres and also historical subjects. Early examples are the portraits of his *Aunt Marianne*, who was murdered in the Nazi euthanasia program because she was an epileptic, or his *Uncle Rudi* in Nazi uniform. With the Nazi doctor *Mr. Heyde,* he also catches one of the perpetrators in picture. The paintings are presented in various shades of grey, and the contours are blurred.

Uncle Rudi, the brother of the artist's mother, stands in the uniform of the *Wehrmacht* in front of a wall that reaches to his neck (Figure 10; 1965). A small tree or shrub rises above its edge. The background is marked by rented flats. The uncle has taken on a relaxed posture. He smiles into the camera. By portraying a member of his family in Nazi uniform – painted after a private photo – Richter reveals the entanglement of an average German family with the Nazi regime. The artist "addresses in a subtle manner questions of collective responsibility and individual guilt of the Germans."[8]

Aunt Marianne, also from the mother's side, is portrayed with the artist himself as a baby, lying with his tummy on a cushion (Figure 11;

---

[8] Dietmar Elger, *Gerhard Richter, Maler*, Köln 2002, 182.

36 God / Terror

Figure 10   Gerhard Richter, *Uncle Rudi*

Guilt, Reconciliation and Grace 37

Figure 11 Gerhard Richter, *Aunt Marianne*

1965). Marianne stands as a young girl behind the furniture, on which the baby lies. Only her torso is visible. She is glancing to the right, while little Gerhard is looking directly at the viewer. The background is bathed in blurred grey tones. Everything is concentrated on the young woman and the child – the Madonna is drawn here into private life.[9] Richter preserves the memory of his aunt, and even turns her into an icon of the victims of the Nazi regime.

Mr. Heyde was one of the leaders of the Nazi euthanasia program. After the war he first lived under a false name in Flensburg and worked as neurologist. He committed suicide before a lawsuit could be filed

---

[9] Richter later painted a cycle with images of his third wife Sabine Moritz and their newborn son that is also reminiscent of portrayals of the Madonna. Today these paintings can be seen in the Kunsthalle in Hamburg. Cf. *Im Blickfeld: Gerhard Richter in der Hamburger Kunsthalle*, with a text by Uwe Schneede, Hamburg 2006.

Werner Heyde im November 1959, als er sich den Behörden stellte.

Figure 12 Gerhard Richter, *Mr. Heyde*

against him as a criminal of war. Behind a police officer, who stands with his back to the camera, the vague facial expressions of a man with thick black spectacles and a hat are visible (Figure 12). The subtitle of the newspaper photo that served as a pattern discloses his identity as "Werner Heyde in November 1959, when he turned himself in to the authorities."[10]

The rift in German society also runs through Richter's own family.[11] While his aunt was murdered by the Nazis, his father and uncle had to serve in the army of the very same Hitler regime. A more fateful irony was that the father of his first wife Ema, Heinrich Eufinger, was one of the key figures in the euthanasia program. After the war he soon became an authority in medical science. For a long time, Richter did not really

---

[10] Elger, *Richter*, 100.

[11] Cf. Jürgen Schreiber, *Ein Maler aus Deutschland. Gerhard Richter. Das Drama einer Familie*, Berlin 2007.

know about this, but in any case he played down the political meaning of his pictures.

> In those days it would have seemed awkward to me to make this background public. Then the artwork would have been seen as reappraisal of contemporary history or social work. [...] Now, I don't mind anymore, if it is known.[12]

With his three paintings that address the Nazi dictatorship Richter, in 1965, was already anticipating the questions of Generation '68. The writer Uwe Timm is one of the most prolific representatives of this generation.[13] Born in 1940, in the midst of World War II, he would later deal in his books with the legacy of the Nazi epoch as well as with the consequences of imperialism and colonialism.[14] Initially, Timm followed in the footsteps of his father, working as a furrier, but went on to study philosophy and literature at university. His single-minded goal was to devote his life to writing. Timm's book *In My Brother's Shadow* (*Am Beispiel meines Bruders*), first published in 2003, addresses questions of guilt and conscience with regard to the years of the Nazi dictatorship from the perspective of the involvement of his own family.

> The stock phrase my parents used for what happened to them was *a blow dealt by fate*, a fate one could not influence. *Our boy and our home both lost*, was one of those sentences that saved you from having to think more deeply about the reasons. And with that suffering you shared in a common atonement. Everything was *horrible* because you yourself were a *victim*, the victim of an inexplicable, collective fate. There were demonic forces that operated beyond history, or were part of human nature. In any case, they were catastrophic and inevitable. Decisions one could only submit to. One felt unjustly treated by fate.[15]

In long flashbacks Timm dissects the life of his parents, searching for their conscience. While his father, according to Timm's observation, tries

---

[12] Quoted by Elger, *Richter*, 172.

[13] Cf. his early *roman a clef* Uwe Timm, *Heißer Sommer*, München 2007⁶ [1974] and its ironic reverberation in Uwe Timm, *Rot*, München 2006⁶ [2001].

[14] Cf. Uwe Timm, *Morenga*, München 1978.

[15] Uwe Timm, *Am Beispiel meines Bruders*, München 2005³, 87f.

to avoid the question of guilt and relativizes it,[16] his mother at least allows it to be asked.[17] With the help of a fragmentary war diary the writer tries to get an impression of his brother, 16 years his senior, who died on the Eastern Front in 1943. The book therefore becomes a requiem.[18] The notes of the brother close with the words: "I close my diary here because I don't see any point in recording the cruel things that sometimes happen."

> I have opened and read this passage time and again while I was writing – it was as if a ray of light was shining in the darkness.
>
> How did he come to this insight? My brother mentions the death of two comrades and the loss of his home. Both events, though, dated from a more distant past. Could it be that in the meantime something happened during his service, something so terrible that it eludes the act of writing? Those brief notes could not convey the suffering, his own or that of others. There is a lack of any compassion – even for himself. And repetition made the futility of it banal, too.
>
> Does this insight, that one cannot keep a record of these cruel things, also extend to foes and victims, the Russian soldiers and civilians? The Jews? The diary contains no anti-Semitic statements or stereotypes, as with the letters of other soldiers from the front: *Untermenschen*, dirt, vermin, Russian clods. On the other hand, there is no show of anything like compassion, no hint of criticism of the circumstances at the time, nothing that would explain a sudden conversion. The notes neither reveal a killer by conviction nor a burgeoning resistance. They show – and that is what is terrifying – a partial blindness, only the *normal* is recorded. All the more astounding are that last sentence and the time lapse between it and the previous entry, *the journey continues*, and the realisation that he is no longer able to write of such *horrible things*. There is the wish, my wish, that this time lapse stands for a No, for the *non servo*, that

---

[16] Timm, *Am Beispiel*, 130; Martin Hielscher, *Uwe Timm*, München 2007, talks about "the Prussian German nationalistic and conservative middle-class values of the father" (cf. ibid., 29).

[17] Timm, *Am Beispiel*, 129.

[18] Hielscher, *Timm*, 177 compares the composition of the book with a fugue. Four times the death of a family member is described, father, mother and the two older siblings, brother and sister. With *Der Freund und der Fremde* Timm followed up with another requiem – for his school friend Benno Ohnesorg, see below (p.67f.).

marks the beginning of a revocation of obedience, that requires more courage than blowing breaches for the tanks to advance. That would be a courage that leads to isolation, that approaches the pride and pain of the man who stands alone.[19]

Timm puts into words – in an often theologically saturated language – what is hidden behind Richter's paintings, the dismay about the banality of evil and the involvement of their own families. Both drag into the light, in their own ways, what still waits to be dealt with.[20]

Similar to Timm, Korean writer Hwang Sok-Yong is also a chronicler of the recent history of his divided country. His novels have an autobiographical touch as well. Born in 1943, in Manchuria, his family fled to the South during the days of the division of the country. He tackles these experiences in his early book *The story of Mr. Han*.[21] In his novel cycle *Chang Kilsan* (1974–1984), originally serialized in a daily newspaper (*Hanguk Ilbo*), Hwang reconstructs Korean history from the perspective of the *Minjung*, the poor, oppressed Korean people. The main character Chang Kilsan is a kind of Korean Robin Hood. The core of the composition is formed around two legends "The falcon of Changsam Cap" and "Chongbul Dong", which both have also been illustrated by Hong Song-Dam.[22]

In 1989 Hwang traveled to the North of the divided country to establish contacts with the writers' organization there. Upon his return from exile in Berlin and New York in 1993 he was sentenced to imprisonment because of an alleged violation of the national security law. After the election of Kim Dae-Jung as president (1998) Hwang was released early from prison with other political prisoners. The parallels to the biography of his fellow countryman Hong Song-Dam are obvious.

In his novel *The Guest*[23] Hwang describes the massacres among North Korean civilians due to the conflicts between Christians and communists in the commotion of the Korean War (1950–53). He also focuses on the fate of two brothers, both Christians, who have been haunted by the ghosts of the past all their lives. The novel is composed in the form of

---

[19] Timm, *Am Beispiel*, 147f. For a reflection on the category courage see above (p.9f. and p.13).

[20] "Only if something is articulated, resistance can emerge" (ibid., 129).

[21] Hwang Sok-Yong, *Die Geschichte des Herrn Han*, München 2005 [Kor. 1972].

[22] Cf. *Malttugi*, 17–22 and 75–83.

[23] Hwang Sok-Yong, *Der Gast*, München 2007 [Engl. 2008].

a shamanist ritual (*Chinogwi-kut*) comprising twelve parts, that is supposed to guide the souls of the deceased safely into the hereafter. The author himself writes:

> I hope that this kind of personal *kut*, can contribute to heal the scars of war that are still visible on the Korean peninsula,[24] the ghosts of cold war find rest and a new century of reconciliation and cooperation may begin.[25]

The younger brother Ryu Yosop, now himself an old man, goes on a trip to his home country. Shortly before his departure his older brother Yohan dies and, as a ghost, accompanies him on his journey into the past. Gradually the events are reconstructed in all their brutality. Not only the two brothers, but also the relatives left behind and the ghosts of the victims, raise their voices. When Yosop visits an uncle, from his mother's side, Ahn Song-Man, called Some, it comes to a catharsis in a big witching hour.

> The other spirits also got up from their places along the wall without any sound and began to disappear in the darkness, suspended like widths of cloth in the wind. From afar a voice said: "The killers and the killed, they all come together again in the other world."
>
> Then it was Yohan, who said to his brother: "Finally I am at home, and finally I can get rid of all the hate and anger, that has been in me for so long, no longer will I wander in a dark foreign land. Take care, you two."
>
> All the ghosts had left. Silence prevailed. Gradually the darkness disappeared, outside the window the silhouettes of the mountains emerged in front of the brightening sky. Nobody was in the room besides Yosop and his uncle.
>
> Uncle Some said: "Those, who had to leave, have gone, now those who are still here have to start anew to live. We have to clean

---

[24] Theologically a similar language game can be found in Dietrich Bonhoeffer, *Ethik*, München 1992, 125–136 esp. 133–136. For Bonhoeffer, justification can only take place within the church, "for the nations there is only the scarification of guilt and the return to order, law and peace." Cf. Magdalene L. Frettlöh, "Der Mensch heißt Mensch, weil er ... vergibt"? Philosophisch-politische und anthropologische Vergebungsdiskurse im Licht der fünften Vaterunserbitte, in: *"Wie? Auch wir vergeben unseren Schuldigern?"*, Jabboq 5, Jürgen Ebach et al. (eds.), Gütersloh 2004, 179–215, 186.

[25] Hwang, Nachwort [Postscript], in: *Der Gast*, 294–297, 297.

the dirt from this stained country, don't you think so?" Yosop folded his hands and started to recite by heart a passage from the Bible [Eccles. 3,8–11].[26]

Besides the division of the country (1945), that resulted in a devastating civil war (1950–53), and the preceding Japanese colonialism (1905/10–45), the period of military dictatorship in the South (1961–88) and the ongoing communist dictatorship in the North is the third traumatic experience for the Korean people to contend with.

Hong Song-Dam also dealt with the Kwangju massacre – by which he himself and Hwang have been traumatized – in an artistic way. The political spring after the assassination of president Park Chung-Hee in 1979 did not last long. Behind the scenes the military quickly became the ruling power. In its internal struggles General Chun Doo-Hwan, who later became president, was already asserting himself over his opponents in December 1979. For the second time after the fall of the Syngman Rhee regime in 1960 caused by student protests, the hopes for democratization were crushed. The disappointed hopes of the people manifested in demonstrations all over the country.

In Kwangju the demonstrators were able to gain temporary control over the city during May 1980. The government sent troops to resolve the conflict. The Special Forces are said to be famished and drugged before the operation. The military acted with brute force against their own community members. The soldiers fired at random into the crowd. Rapes and cruel mutilations in public occurred. The officers in charge, Chun Doo-Hwan and Rho Tae-Woo, both later became presidents.[27] The American supreme command must have agreed to the deployment, or at least tolerated it, because temporarily troops had to be withdrawn from the 38th Parallel to the interior of the country.[28] Kwangju remained a collective trauma for the Korean people for a long time. A volume with woodcuts of Hong Song-Dam, published in 1990 in Korea contains 50 prints originating from the past decade gathered under the title "Kwangju."[29]

---

[26] Hwang, *Der Gast*, 285.

[27] Chun (b. 1931; in office 1980–88) and Rho (b. 1932; 1988–93).

[28] Only on December 1, 1994, after 44 years, was peace-time operational control over the Korean troops returned from the US to Korea. The wartime command is reserved by the Americans for themselves even today.

[29] Cf. the catalogue *Prints of Hong Seong-Dam*, Seoul 1990.

"Memory" is a central category in the works of all the artists introduced here. With his Baader-Meinhof cycle *October 18, 1977* Gerhard Richter sparked heated debates even a decade after the so-called "German Autumn".[30] The artist tackles the death of the core members of the Red Army Faction in the high-security wing of the Stammheim prison which was erected especially for them. Richter, who earlier failed artistically to depict the horror of the Nazi concentration camps,[31] undertakes with these paintings another attempt to meet the aesthetic challenge of depicting the horrible in an artistic way.

> Actually, I have painted just the un-paintable pictures. The dead. In the beginning I wanted to depict the whole problem, the reality of that time, the vivid – I thought more about something big, all-encompassing regarding this theme. But then it went into another direction namely towards death. And that is not so unpaintable after all, on the contrary, death and suffering have always been a theme of art.[32]

Emerging from the protest movements of the restorative post-war Germany – against rearmament, the Vietnam war and for reforms in higher education – the members of what was to become the Baader-Meinhof group increasingly isolated themselves with a growing willingness to use violence. With the liberation of Andreas Baader, who had been imprisoned

---

[30] Cf. Robert Storr, *Gerhard Richter October 18, 1977*, New York 2000; Stefan Aust, *Der Baader Meinhof Komplex*, Hamburg 1986.

[31] Cf. Elger, *Richter*, 371. With *Birkenau* (2014) Richter in the meantime has succeeded in a convincing adaptation of the theme. It is a complex retouch of four shadowy photographs, snapshots of the genocide, taken clandestinely by a special command of Jewish KZ inmates. The grey tones changing between white and black, covering the images like ashes, are ruptured by the underlying layers of bloody red and bilious green tones. The four large-sized canvases count for Richter as one image. He took photographs of them again and installed them at their original size behind acrylic glass – from photograph to retouched painting to photograph. The artist also published a book with 93 detailed photographs of his retouche (Gerhard Richter, *Birkenau*, Köln 2015). The Museum Frieda Burda in Baden-Baden documented this multilayered process in one gallery space so that the images could draw the beholder into their dialogue. Cf. *Gerhard Richter. Birkenau*, Helmut Friedel (ed.), Köln 2016.

[32] Quoted in Elger, *Richter*, 371.

because of arson in a department store in Frankfurt[33] during a furlough in 1970, their journey into the underground began. After only two years however, which they spent mainly in criminal activities to sustain their illegal life in hiding – bank robbery, car and weapon theft – the protagonists of the first generation were captured. What followed then was a self-referential *danse macabre*, which centered on a single goal: the freeing of their comrades from prison.[34] There was no practical engagement whatsoever with the victims of the Nazi dictatorship or those of imperialism and colonialism.[35] On the contrary, the cooperation with the Palestinian franc-tireurs for instance was also directed against Israel.

In the case of the kidnapping of the chairman of the Berlin CDU, Peter Lorenz, in 1975 by members of the "movement June 2 (*Bewegung '2. Juni'*)" the West German government complied with their demands and flew six terrorists to Aden in exchange. Yet afterwards it changed its policy to one of no tolerance. Both in the case of the occupation of the German embassy in Stockholm in 1975, as well as the kidnapping of the chairman of the employers' organization Hans Martin Schleyer and the accompanying high jacking of an airplane[36] in 1977, negotiations were only entered into as a pretence to gain time.

Hans Martin Schleyer, formerly a bona fide Nazi, at least fit the profile of the enemy as formulated by Gudrun Enslin.[37] Stefan Aust relates that on the occasion of the assassination of Benno Ohnesorg she exclaimed: "This fascist state intends to kill us all. We must organize resistance. Violence can only be answered with violence. This is the generation of

---

[33] Following the example of a similar action in Brussels (1967) – which was propagated in a flyer by the members of the Berlin-based 'Commune I' as a suitable form of protest against the Vietnam War – Baader and Gudrun Enslin together with Thorwald Proll and Horst Söhnlein set fire to two department stores in Frankfurt (1968). Yet, unlike in Brussels, no human lives were lost.

[34] The Terror commandos often bore the names of comrades who were dead or imprisoned.

[35] The theologian Helmut Gollwitzer, who probably dealt most profoundly with the RAF, makes a point. Cf. Jörg Hermann, "Unsere Söhne und Töchter" Protestantismus und RAF-Terrorismus in den 1970er Jahren, in: Kraushaar, *RAF*, Bd. 1, 644–656, esp. 652–655.

[36] On October 13, 1977, Palestinian franc-tireurs highjacked the Lufthansa aircraft *Landshut* that took off in Palma de Mallorca, in order to support the demands of their German comrades.

[37] Cf. the statement of his son Hans-Eberhard Schleyer, in: Anne Siemens, *Für die RAF war er das System, für mich der Vater. Die andere Geschichte des deutschen Terrorismus*, München 2007, 127–183, esp. 171 and 175.

Auschwitz – one cannot argue with them!"[38] The other victims seem to be picked more or less arbitrarily as representatives of the "pig system (*Schweinesystem*)", as the terrorists used to call it. Often, they came from the same liberal bourgeois milieu as the terrorists themselves. "The revolution ate its parents." Most obvious is the case of Jürgen Ponto, who opened the door to his slayers; because the befriended couple of lawyers Albrecht had announced the imminent visit of their daughter Susanne – Ponto's godchild – by phone. After the collective suicide of the leadership of the first generation in Stammheim – staged to appear as a possible assassination by agents of the state and readily seized upon by the media[39] – the terrorists had lost their apparently primary goal, the liberation of the prisoners, and started to kill at random.

Most of the RAF cadre were from middle-class backgrounds, many were academically trained. Some of them had grown up in protestant vicarages or were socialized in church circles.[40] The partial success of the Confessing Church in resisting the Nazi regime was followed by rebellion against the Vietnam War, which was perceived as a new, more violent injustice. "The topic of resistance was [...] a central moment of continuity between left wing Protestantism, the student movement and RAF-terrorism."[41] All this led to several attempts from representatives of the political left[42] as well as theologians[43] to enter into dialogue with the terrorists after their imprisonment, yet without success. Richter, who mistrusted any ideology and rejected the deeds of the terrorists, was at the same time fascinated by their consequence and courage.

> Coming from the GDR at the beginning of the 60s, I refused naturally to be appreciative of the aims and methods of the RAF. I was indeed impressed by the energy, the uncompromising will and

---

[38] Aust, *Baader Meinhof Komplex*, 54.

[39] Parallels can be drawn with 9/11 as a media event; see above (p.6f.).

[40] Cf. Wolfgang Huber in the *Tagespiegel* on 12.02.2007: "Our church was, for better or worse, also a part of the movement 68."

[41] Hermann, "Unsere Söhne und Töchter", 647 cf. 649.

[42] Regarding the visit the French philosopher Jean Paul Satre paid Andreas Baader in Stammheim cf. Ruud Welten, *Zinvol Geweld. Satre, Camus en Merlau-Ponty over terreur en terrorisme*, Kampen 2006.

[43] The protestant theologians Helmut Gollwitzer, Heinrich Albertz and Martin Niemöller, polemically labeled as "gang of three", were severely insulted for their pastoral efforts in the so called "Berlin church controversy". Cf. Hermann, "Unsere Söhne und Töchter".

the downright grit of the terrorists, but I could not hold its rigidity against the state; States are like that and I experienced other, more remorseless ones.[44]

This ambivalence in Richter's attitude has its parallels in the statements by Karl-Heinz Stockhausen and Susan Sontag regarding the assassins of 9/11.[45] At the same time Richter never tires of emphasizing that he took up the subject out of mere aesthetic interest:

The political relevance of my "October paintings" does not interest me so much; yet in many reviews that is the one and only thing that is of any interest. According to the actual political circumstances the pictures are received in one way or the other. I find that rather disturbing.[46]

Kaja Silverman connects *Betty*, a portrait of Richter's daughter from 1977, with his later portraits of Gudrun Enslin and Ulrike Meinhof.[47] This would point to a long-standing examination of the problem. The similarities in clothing, expression and posture as well as composition referred to by Silverman are evident. Elger[48] and Storr[49] refer furthermore to another picture of his daughter painted a decade later while Richter was working on the Baader-Meinhof cycle. The colorful painting, showing his daughter in spring-like clothing with her face turned away from the viewer, stands in sharp contrast with the black and white pictures of the Baader-Meinhof cycle, as well as with the thought-provoking early portrait (*Betty, 1977*). Betty gazes into the green-grayish background as into a dark mirror. For a moment it seems to resemble the youthful portrait of Ulrike Meinhof, which itself does not fit at all into the rest of the Baader-Meinhof cycle.[50] Richter himself denies any connection: "No, nothing. It was only interesting to me, that the portrait of Ulrike Meinhof was so

---

[44] Richter quoted in Elger, *Richter*, 380.

[45] See above (p.13).

[46] Quoted in op. cit., 357.

[47] *Documenta 12 Kassel 16/06–23/09, 2007. Katalog*, Köln 2007, 104f.

[48] Cf. op. cit., 383.

[49] Cf. Storr, *October 18*, 134.

[50] Cf. Elger, *Richter*, 381.

much better than this painting."⁵¹ In his *catalogue raisonné* the artist has interestingly enough "moved it a couple of numbers away from the cycle, out of the sequence of its creation".⁵²

The clue to these interconnections in Richter's oeuvre seems to lie in his aversion to everything ideological. From his own experience, he is aware of the vulnerability of human beings to ideological seduction. With regard to the Nazi period he had already represented this on the familial level. In the youth portrait of Ulrike Meinhof and the two portraits of his own daughter the question seems to flash up again: whether or not any human being can come into the maelstrom of an ideology. For the sake of the universal validity of this insight, Richter eventually sold the paintings to the Museum of Modern Art in New York.⁵³

> Probably the Americans because of their distance from the RAF view more the common aspects of the theme that concerns nearly every modern or even non-modern country: the general danger of being ideology prone, of fanaticism and madness.⁵⁴

Richter finally chose 15 paintings from a larger number, which he had drawn in a nine month period between February and November 1988.⁵⁵

---

⁵¹ Quoted op. cit., 383.

⁵² Ibid.

⁵³ After the paintings had received an initial, critical reception in Germany, their sale abroad also provoked criticism. All of a sudden, they were regarded as belonging to Germany.

⁵⁴ Richter quoted in Elger, *Richter*, 384 (cf. 381). Yet perhaps Richter is underestimating the significance of contextuality, in the MoMA the paintings are predominantly kept in the depot. During a visit in November 2013 the whole cycle was on display. The visitors however just passed by this particular gallery.

⁵⁵ "What did I paint. Three times Baader shot down, two times Enslin hanged, three times the head of the dead Meinhof taken down from her gallows, one time the dead Meins. Three times Enslin, indifferent (reminiscent of a popstar). Then a big, vacuous funeral – a prison cell, dominated by a bookshelf – a silent, grey record player – a youth portrait of Meinhof, bourgeois sentimental – two times the arrest of Meins, who has to surrender to the concentrated power of the state. All paintings are vague, grey, most of the time very blurred, diffuse. They represent the horror and the refusal of an answer, an explanation or opinion that is hard to bear. I am not sure, whether the pictures 'ask for something' rather they provoke objection because of their hopelessness and desolateness, because of their impartialness." Diary entry of Richter dating December 7, 1988, quoted by Elger, *Richter*, 359. Later Richter painted over three of the paintings mentioned in an abstract manner (cf. op. cit., 362).

Guilt, Reconciliation and Grace 49

They have no fixed sequence. Some of the paintings show the same photo in different details or the same subject in changing perspectives: *Arrest 1–2* of Holger Meins, *Confrontation 1–3* with Gudrun Enslin, *Enslin Hanged*, Andreas Baader as *Man Shot Down 1–2* and *Ulrike Meinhof Dead 1–3*. The grey tones preferred by Richter are supposed to create distance from the subject.

> Grey. It does not contain any message. It does not evoke feelings or associations; it is neither visible nor invisible. Its inconspicuousness gives it the capacity to mediate, to make visible in a positive illusionistic manner, like a photo. It has a capacity to make "nothing" visible, that no other color has. Grey is for me the welcome and in fact only possible equivalent for indifference, not being involved, absence of opinion and absence of form.[56]

The artist takes the freedom to touch up and blur. He seems to zoom in and out. This artistic strategy crosses, in a sense, the borders between photo and film. The sequence of the three Enslin paintings for example shows her appearing from the left in the first picture, looking directly into the camera in the second and then, in the third, exiting to the right with her head bowed. Already the chosen subjects and titles are reminiscent of elements of the passion story, *arrest* in Gethsemane, *confrontation* with Pilate and the people of Jerusalem, *hanged* on the cross, *dead* and *funeral*.

The surprising formal parallels with Hong Song-Dam's *Kwangju* cycle, which are discussed in the following comparisons, should not deceive: that here victims of the South Korean state terrorism are contrasted with failed terrorists, who declared war on a democratically elected government.

Hanged

The shadowy picture shows Gudrun Enslin hanged at the bars of her prison cell window (Figure 13). Nine months previously Ulrike Meinhof had hung herself at the very same window. In the large, subdivided opening, the middle section stands wide open, giving access to the bars outside. Enslin's facial expression cannot be identified. Against the original photo, and what is physically and anatomically possible, the dead woman seems to have turned away her head from potential beholders. Her extremities

---

[56] Richter quoted in Storr, *October 18*, 112.

50   *God / Terror*

Figure 13   Gerhard Richter, *Hanged*

become blurred in the gray tones of the composition, which turn into black towards the left margin of the picture.

Traveling in disguise 3

A person is hung up with his wrists tied together above his head (Figure 14). Under his ruffled hair his gaze is grim. Stubbly beard and tattered clothing point to a life full of privation. The black background is only interrupted by a white flash directly above the figure. Hong's series

Guilt, Reconciliation and Grace 51

Figure 14   Hong Song-Dam, *Traveling in disguise*

Traveling in disguise tries to draw a connection between the Kwangju massacre and the Tonghak rebellion against Japanese colonialism.⁵⁷

---

⁵⁷ Tonghak is a New Korean Religion that fuses elements from Confucianism, Buddhism and Taoism to counter colonialism. Shamanist and Christian elements can also be traced. Cf. Benjamin B. Weems, *Reforms, Rebellion and the Heavenly Way*, Tucson, Arizona 1964; Yong Choon Kim, *The Ch'ondogyo Concept of Man. An Essence of Korean Thought*, Seoul 1978; Sung-Soo Kim, *Die Tonghak-Bewegung in Korea. Sozio-ökonomische Hintergründe und ideologischer Wandlungsprozeß*, Dissertation, Frankfurt a.M. 1980; Ok Soong Won-Cha, *Der Einfluß der Donghak-Bewegung auf die Ausbildung der Minjung-Theologie in Korea*, Dissertation, Frankfurt a.M. 1986.

52   God / Terror

Man shot down

The dead Baader lies on the floor (Figure 15). His head is bent over strangely in a puddle of blood. The right arm is laid against the body while the outstretched left arm hangs down loosely. The position of his body is reminiscent of a pietà without Mary holding him on her lap.[58]

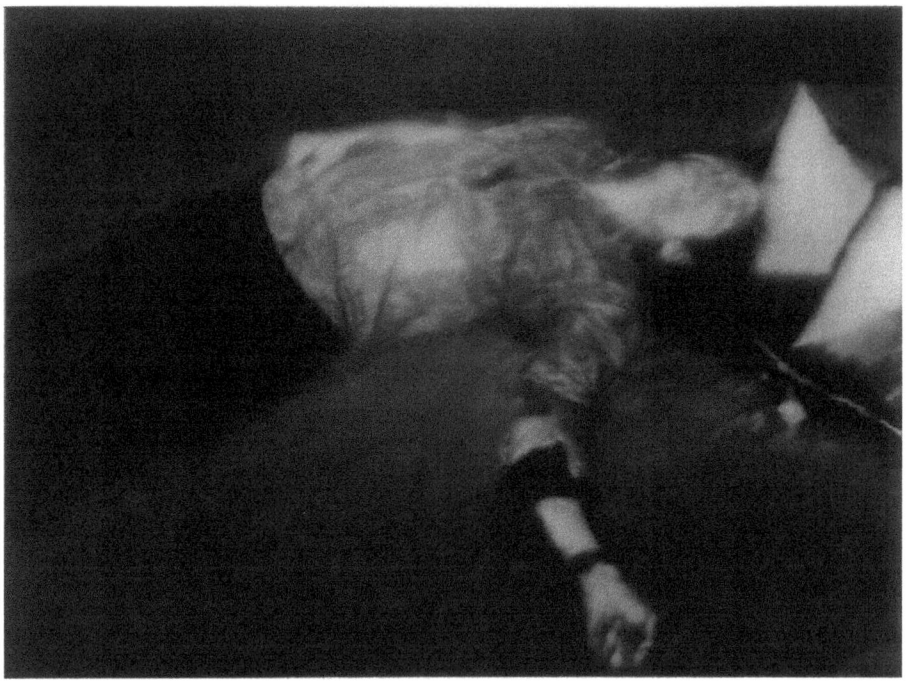

Figure 15   Gerhard Richter, *Man Shot Down*

Blood and tears 7

In a puddle of blood lies the dead body of a woman (Figure 16). Her blouse is torn, one breast is exposed. She shares the fate of many women who have been raped before being murdered during the Kwangju massacre by relentless soldiers, their own countrymen.

---

[58] Cf. Storr, *October 18*, 123 (cf. 108) points to the similarity with the historical painting *Death of Marat* by Jaques-Louis David and his allusion to the *Pietà* of Michelangelo.

Guilt, Reconciliation and Grace 53

Figure 16   Hong Song-Dam, *Blood and Tears 7*

Dead

In the style of a portrait the picture shows only the head and shoulders of the dead Ulrike Meinhof – cut down from her self-chosen gallows – in front of a nearly black background (Figure 17). The strangulation marks around her neck are clearly visible. Associations with the pedrella *Christ in the tomb* (1521/22) by Franz Holbein the Younger (1497–1543) come to the fore.[59]

My name is

Under a traditional grass mount somewhere in the hills around Kwangju the upper part of a dead body is visible (Figure 18). Nobody is there, even to close his eyes that have seen so much injustice. Still he wants to be called by his name, not to be forgotten.

---

[59] In the permanent collection of the Kunsthalle Basel.

54   *God / Terror*

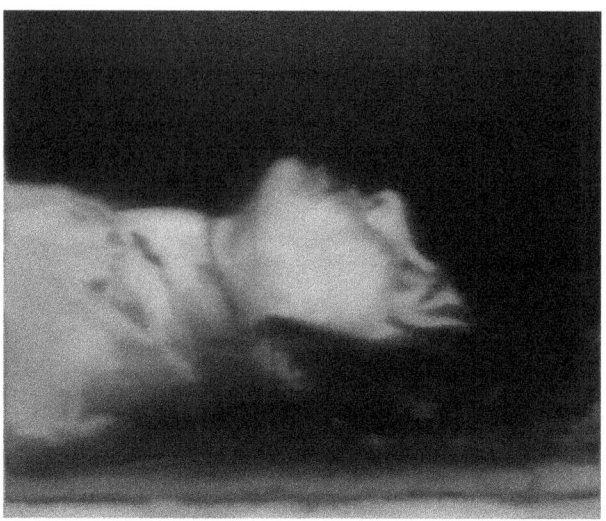

Figure 17   Gerhard Richter, *Dead*

Figure 18   Hong Song-Dam, *My Name Is*

Figure 19   Gerhard Richter, *Funeral*

Funeral

The coffins of Baader, Enslin and Jan-Carl Raspe are escorted by a crowd in the cemetery *Waldfriedhof* in Stuttgart (Figure 19). The picture is structured by the diagonal line of the three coffins and another one in the right corner, together forming a kind of T-cross.[60] The cross-form reoccurs among the trees on the horizon[61] that is usually quite decisive for Richter's paintings. The then mayor of Stuttgart, Christian democrat Manfred Rommel (1928–2013), a devout Christian, opposed those voices in the general public, who objected to burying them in a cemetery, with the statement "All enmity should cease after death."[62]

---

[60] This second diagonal element, modified by Richter, is not identifiable in the original photograph (cf. op. cit., 113).

[61] Cf. op. cit., 109. The three crosses are not perceptible in the original photograph (cf. op. cit., 113).

[62] Quoted op. cit., 64.

Kwangju

In a woodcut by Hong Song-Dam the crucifixion appears only as a torso in the lower third of the picture (Figure 20), in its center, however, there is a lorry with three bodies on the open platform. They almost appear like sacks – carelessly hurled down: human material in complete disregard of human dignity. On their hands and feet, they bear the stigmata of Jesus Christ. The background of the picture is black, interrupted only by a couple of lines in the upper right corner, which apparently are supposed to represent the outline of mountains.

Hong uses the crucifixion as a powerful symbol of identification for those who are suffering themselves. The conviction of faith that God is present amidst human suffering gives hope against all hope and empowers the downtrodden to become agents of change. From a theological point of view Richter gives artistic form to a "way of the cross" or a passion play.[63] The perpetrators have in the end become victims of their own ideology. The passion story also creates space to thematize human failure and guilt. Resurrection may be distant, but still reconciliation seems possible in the shadowy depiction of the cross.[64] Johann Baptist Metz's critical reference to the "soteriological circle", "in which the biblical question of justice for the innocent suffering is changed too quickly […] into the question of redemption for the perpetrators"[65], is directed against wrong theological thinking and human behavior. Metz certainly does not deny God the possibility of granting grace freely.

Hong Song-Dam, as with Hwang Sok-Yong, was persecuted after the official end of the military dictatorship on grounds of the security laws which were still valid. Both were accused of having illegal contacts with North Korea. In the 1990s Hong Song-Dam tried to cope with his prison experience in an artistic way, as he did with the Kwangju massacre in

---

[63] Storr, (*October 18*, 110) interprets the three crosses on the horizon of the funeral painting as "a discrete benediction at the end of a modern-day passion play which, in its scrupulous and agonizing rendition, offers no other consolation". It is worth noting that the curator of the Museum for Modern Art in New York repeatedly refers to Christianity in regard to these paintings.

[64] Cf. Storr, *October 18*, 105: "No crucifixion or deposition was ever more morbid, […]. In these paintings, however, there is no hope, no resurrection, only numbing finality."

[65] Metz, *Memoria*, 10 fn. 13; cf. 57; see below (p.73).

Guilt, Reconciliation and Grace 57

Figure 20 Hong Song-Dam, *Kwangju*

Figure 21 Hong Song-Dam, *The twenty days in water* (1)

the 1980s.[66] However, he switched his technique from woodprint to oil painting.[67] Born on an island surrounded by water the artist strives to gain back the positive memories of experiencing life at the seaside in his youth after being exposed to water torture during his imprisonment. The guards forced liters of water down his throat and pressed his head under water for several minutes. In the series *The twenty days in water* (8 pieces; 1999) Hong describes the metamorphosis of the one tortured with water into a fish, which cannot live without water.

---

[66] Cf. Resistance and Meditation. Hong Sung-Dam, in: *EAST Wind*, New York 2003.

[67] The mural style of the protest years is resumed by Hong in a number of oversized oil paintings. After earlier tableaus denouncing the ecological crisis in more recent works, he has created mytho-poetic worlds, mixing elements of Korean history and culture with fantasy.

Guilt, Reconciliation and Grace   59

The first image of the series (Figure 21; 650×530 mm) shows the victim naked, tied to a chair, upside down, drowning in water. Flowers are blossoming from the legs of the chair, which are just sticking out of the water. The victim's feet are tied to the front chair legs. The flowers pictured grow only in coastal areas. In the moment close to death, when the torture has reached a point where resistance fades, Hong recalls these flowers of his youth. In the early morning hours, when fog is covering the ground up to one's knees, the flowers seem to drift on the sea. Even these beautiful flowers have forsaken him in his own perception. Beside the chair a rice bowl floats on the water. While for his friend and companion, the poet Kim Chi-Ha, rice as the basic food of many Asian countries is a symbol of life, Hong Song-Dam has a much more ambivalent notion of it. One can only be tortured if one has enough to eat. Rice then becomes part of the torture process. This insight is hidden behind the third painting

Figure 22   Hong Song-Dam, *The twenty days in water* (3)

of the series. Its focus is a white tray with a simple Korean meal – rice, soup and kimchi – as it is still delivered today in Seoul from the local cookshop (Figure 22). In the lower part of the painting, also in white, the upper part of the prisoner's head is to be seen, his eyes are closed. The painting catches the moment when he is dunked into the water head first. In front of his inner eye the aforementioned meal appears.

In the first image, meanwhile, fish are swimming around the body that is floating in the water. On the right hand a single tree grows on the cliffs. In the upper left corner one can see a distant island, reminiscent of the artist's own home island Haui.

The second image of the series also shows the process of water torture (Figure 23). On first viewing the face of the artist seems to mirror itself

Figure 23   Hong Song-Dam, *The twenty days in water* (2)

Guilt, Reconciliation and Grace 61

Figure 24   Hong Song-Dam, *The twenty days in water* (4)

in the washbasin, with soap and a toothbrush lying at the fringe. Yet the facial features are missing and the skin is strangely discolored, a sign of the impending death by asphyxiation. Around his neck the water is frizzing on closer examination. The shoulders seem restrained, probably because the arms are tied to the body.

In the fourth picture (Figure 24; 650×530 mm) the former prisoner has grown fins and is swimming with a fish. Together their bodies form a circle, reminisced of the *yin-yang* symbol of cosmic harmony. Only the face with eyes closed looms out of the water on the fifth picture

62   God / Terror

Figure 25   Hong Song-Dam, *The twenty days in water* (5)

(Figure 25; 650×530 mm). The artist has painted flowers and trees on his forehead. His thoughts roam to the nature that only can be sustained by water.

For the last three pictures Hong chooses the shape of a *mandala*. In number six (Figure 26; 1200×1200 mm) man and fish circle around the chair, with some of the bonds hanging over the backrest. In the seventh picture (Figure 27; 1200×1200 mm) they are surrounded by depictions of memories from the artist's life. Close to death one's life passes before the inner eye. The two are now swimming around a rice bowl. In the concluding picture (Figure 28; 1200×1200 mm) the man is completely

Guilt, Reconciliation and Grace   63

Figure 26   Hong Song-Dam, *The twenty days in water* (6)

Figure 27   Hong Song-Dam, *The twenty days in water* (7)

64   *God / Terror*

Figure 28   Hong Song-Dam, *The twenty days in water* (8)

transformed into a fish. The two fish still circle around the rice bowl, the color of which has changed from the yellow hue of the preceding picture to pure white, symbol of catharsis.[68]

Hong Song-Dam has recovered from his trauma through his artwork. One of the torturers who was tracked down by an investigative TV program showed no repentance, and even said that they obviously did not torture him enough because he is still politically active. While Hong Song-Dam has gone through a process of aesthetic self-reconciliation, mutual reconciliation and forgiveness have not even begun in Korea.[69]

---

[68] In the series *Meals* of 68 square paintings in mixed media Hong has created variations on the rice bowl, given to him through a square hole at the bottom of his prison wall (cf. the painting *Distributing meals*, in: *EAST Wind*, 67).

[69] Cf. Chai Soo-Il, Die Überwindung der Gewalt aus der Sicht der Opfer – Das Beispiel von Hong Sung Dam, in: Benjamin Simon and Henning Wrogemann (eds.), *Konviviale*

In his novel *The Old Garden*[70] Hwang Sok-Yong describes the difficult way of the long-term political prisoner, Oh Hyunuh, returning to the freedom for which he once fought. This fictive character serves as an example for the experience of Hwang, Hong and many other South Koreans, who were imprisoned and tortured because of their peaceful engagement for democratization and reunification. With the help of the letters and diaries of his fiancé Han Yunhi, who has died of cancer during his imprisonment, Hyunuh opens up the lost years for himself and at the same time remembers the past. This becomes symbolically visible in a double portrait that she painted of them both, which is mentioned several times in the story line. Only after being released from prison does our protagonist hear from his sister that Yunhi has died. She hands over to Hyunuh the letters from Yunhi that did not reach him in prison. All that remains for him is the memory of the months they shared in a hut in Galmoe, a village in the vincity of Kwangju. The teacher Yunhi, herself the daughter of a communist, has offered him, the politically haunted, a place to hide from the police. In her last letter to him she writes:

> After leaving Galmoe I once painted your young face. Later I draw my own self which has grown old on the margins. Suddenly you looked as if you were my son. [...] You had a life in there and I had one outside. Even though our days were quite hard, we should reconcile with them (44).

Homeless as he is Hyunuh sets off on a journey into their common past. In the small hut – that Yunhi bought before her death, to leave behind at least a place for her lover and that still is maintained by their former landlady – he finds her diaries and the painting:

> I draw forth one of the paintings and put it on the empty easel. Two faces were depicted on the picture – one big, the other small. The left one was mine. In the picture I was wearing a blue-white checkered, short-sleeved shirt. It was my last summer of freedom. In those days everybody was wearing long hair. My hair was also

---

Theologie, Festgabe für Theo Sundermeier zum 70. Geburtstag, Frankfurt a.M. 2005, 287–298. Krog, *Country*, 220 documents similar experiences of victims of the apartheid regime: "The point of the TRC is to enable healing to happen. And let it be said that here in me there is at least one person they have helped to reconcile: myself to myself."

[70] Hwang Sok-Yong, *Der ferne Garten*, München 2005 [Engl. 2012]; page references in the text.

> covering the collar. Around the eyes a dark shadow was drawn; the cavernous cheeks seemed to express my suffering. The background was painted in a dark red basic tint; the China blue, painted at right angles, emphasized the sad mood even more. The lattice window pasted with paper next to my face was covered with grey color by Yunhi and then – that's how she described it in her letter to me – she has drawn her own portrait upon it. Only now I saw the face of her last years. She has painted over it several times with crude and broad strokes. Her hair was partly grey and the eyes were only painted in black, so that one could hardly detect the expression behind them. The cheeks themselves were painted over with different colors. She was no young woman anymore. Still her peculiar smile, that one could hardly assess, was clearly recognizable in the fine contours of her lips. She looked at me quiescently with this smile, that I loved so much. A young man, thirty-two years of age and a woman in her forties were looking at me (76f.).

Through Yunhi's notes Hyunuh also gets to know about their daughter, who was raised by her sister. Besides the hut in Galmoe the daughter is the only lasting connection between the two lovers: "While I was convinced, that nothing remained of her, Yunhi has in fact left this child behind" (173). The end of the book leaves unresolved, whether the father succeeds in establishing a lasting relationship with his now 17-year-old daughter. From Galmoe he seems in any case to have already taken his leave, with a last look at the painting.

> Now I am looking again at my young face that Yunhi left behind in Galmoe. [...] In the period between the middle of July until the beginning of August, when she painted that image, most of the time tense silence prevailed between us. Still we always were very close to each other. Sometimes she was smiling so strangely, and all the time she seemed as if she wanted to say something. If I recall this now, she did not look alone at me, but together with the child. At the place were originally the lattice window was, she painted her face. Her distinctive cheekbones, the crinkles around her eyes and her hair that started to turn grey, made her look lonely. Her eyes however attested to a deep inner peace, just like her warm smile. The young man of thirty-two and the woman in her forties seemed to look out of the picture into the real world. Standing behind me, she loomed over my shoulder. In what direction did the path lead

that my young, passionate self had chosen – and that she should see over my shoulder only much later with her own eyes (238f.)?

In his novel *The friend and the stranger*[71] Uwe Timm also deals with his experience of the student movement, when he recalls his friendship with Benno Ohnesorg, who was killed by policeman Karl-Heinz Kurras during the demonstrations against the state visit of the shah of Persia Reza Pachlevi[72] in 1967. His death triggered in a certain sense the German student movement[73] that turned against the ongoing western imperialism in the Global South as well as the repression of the German Nazi past. Timm had lost contact with the friend of his youth many years before. He hears about his death on the radio while he is studying in Paris. Only decades later is the writer able to compose this requiem[74] on this person from the long-gone days of his youth. Again, the image of a man and a woman – this time a photo – is central to remembering the past.

> He has made a difference – as victim. The photo that shows him lying on the ground that could be seen in all newspapers, that was reprinted time and again, that I saw in Paris. This young woman bends over him, holding his head, the blood on the ground, this photo has caused outrage, like only pictures can do. [...]
> The photo, that shows him lying on the ground dying, accumulates Christian motives. This woman, in a festive black cape, leaving the arms free, kneeling next to him; her gaze directed upwards to the right. The association is obvious: a religious icon. Does she talk to somebody? Does she ask for something? This picture shows the situation of sacrifice. Also, the despair in regard to the powerlessness over the factual, the violence, the death, all that transformed the existing, pent up reluctance in the will to act. The time

---

[71] Uwe Timm, *Der Freund und der Fremde*, München 2007.

[72] Mohammed Reza Pachlevi who came to power in 1941 after his father had resigned established a pro-western anti-communist regime, what guaranteed him the support of the US. Cf. Bahmãn Nirumand, *Persien, Modell eines Entwicklungslandes oder Die Diktatur der Freien Welt*, Hamburg 1967, a popular book in the student movement, that was also found in the bequest of Benno Ohnesorg.

[73] The self-immolation of worker Chun Tae-Il (1971) protesting against the inhuman working conditions in the textile industry had a similar function for the South Korean student movement.

[74] See above the earlier family requiem *Am Beispiel meines Bruders* (pp.39–41).

was as we say ripe. In order for such thunderstorms to happen, a special occasion is necessary, a special person, a special image that anchors in consciousness that loads the cognition with emotion that on its part lightens analytically acquired knowledge.[75]

Timm, who identifies himself as an agnostic, reveals the religious connotations of this icon of Generation '68. He refers to the *pietà* and talks about sacrifice in recollection of the traditional interpretation of the death of Jesus Christ on the cross: "the sacrificial death, a death that spares others from death."[76]

Religiously inspired iconography, whether icons of the victims or triptychs of the stories of martyrdom, that includes the perpetrators was instrumental also in the struggle against the South African apartheid regime, and later the reappraisal of its consequences.[77] Officially introduced in 1948,[78] apartheid was an attempt to decree the segregation of the races by law. With the release of Nelson Mandela (1918–2013), the charismatic president of the African National Congress (ANC) in 1990, who had been imprisoned since 1962, the gradual abolition of apartheid began. In 1994 this process was crowned with the first free elections. Yet the black population is still suffering from the effects of apartheid. Land reform and the payment of reparations are progressing rather slowly.

The ANC suffered from a tremendous loss of popularity under president Jacob Zuma (b. 1942; in office 2009–2018).[79] The corruption of the black power elite has led the richest and most developed country on the African continent to the brink. Even among the staunch support in the townships finally opposition was growing. Liberation theologians, who temporarily served in the government, like Frank Chicane (b. 1951), bring bitter charges against their former comrades-in-arms. Whether the will for self-purification is strong enough and president Cyril Ramaphosa (b. 1952; since 2018), who also belongs to the old ANC guard, can regain

---

[75] Timm, *Der Freund*, 117f.

[76] Op. cit., 113.

[77] Cf. John W. de Gruchy, *Christianity, Art and Transformation. Theological Aesthetics in the Struggle for Justice*, Cambridge, New York 2001.

[78] It was however already implicit in the passport laws the British passed in 1931, which stipulated, that non-Whites always had to carry a passport on them, from which was apparent, where they were allowed to be, and when.

[79] From 62% of the votes in the election of Nelson Mandela as first non-white president of South Africa in 1994 to 54.5 % in the local elections 2016.

lost terrain and change course, only time will tell. The South African post-apartheid democracy is on trial.

With her *Truth Game Series* Sue Williamson grapples with the work of the South African Truth and Reconciliation Commission (TRC).[80] In the form of a triptych the different pieces of the series show in the left third a relative of the victim and in the right third one of the perpetrators who has been involved in the case. In the center is either a portrait of the victim or images related to the circumstances of the deed. Ten parallel rails with the same space in between have been attached to each painting. On these devices the viewers can move colored Plexiglas elements back and forth, on which text fragments from the transcripts of the hearings are imprinted. By doing so they are included in the search for truth.

The picture *Nkosinathi Biko – False medical certificate – Dr. Benjamin Tucker* (Figure 29) for example depicts Steve Biko's[81] son Nkosinathi on the left, and on the right the then medical officer in charge, who signed the death certificate, which certified a natural cause of death. Both wear headphones which was a common practice during the hearings because of the differing language worlds. On the moveable Plexiglas elements one can read the following text fragments from top down: "death in detention", "examined repeatedly", "father's brain hemorrhage", "Bantu Stephen Biko", the name of the victim, "false medical certificate", "what happened in room 619" and "disgraceful conduct". The way in which the artist talks about her work, reminds one on the criterion of *distance* introduced in part one:

---

[80] The establishment of the TRC had been decided in 1995 after long negotiations between the African National Congress (ANC) and the National Party of the Boers. The basic idea of the *Promotion of National Unity and Reconciliation Act 34* of 1995 is that those who confess their deeds, that where politically motivated, can apply for amnesty. The commission had three subcommittees, that were dealing with gross human rights violations, amnesty and reparations as well as rehabilitations. The human rights committee finished its work back in 1997, the amnesty committee continued until 2001. Most of the criticism focused on the failure to pay reparations. Cf. Charles Villa-Vincencio and Wilhelm Verwoerd (eds.), *Looking Back Reaching Forward. Reflections on the Truth and Reconciliation Commission of South Africa*, London and New York 2000.

[81] Steve Biko (1946–1977) was co-founder of the *South African Student Organization* (SASO) in 1968, and its first president. His slogan "black is beautiful" identifies him as thinker in the tradition of Frantz Fanon. The black population has to overcome the internalized perspective of the oppressors. He planted the seed for the *Black Consciousness Movement* (BCM). Cf. Steve Biko, *I Write What I Like*, Johannesburg 2004 [London 1978]. Biko was banned by the apartheid regime in 1973. After being arrested in 1977, he died a couple of days later due to heavy head injuries, caused by his torturers.

70 *God / Terror*

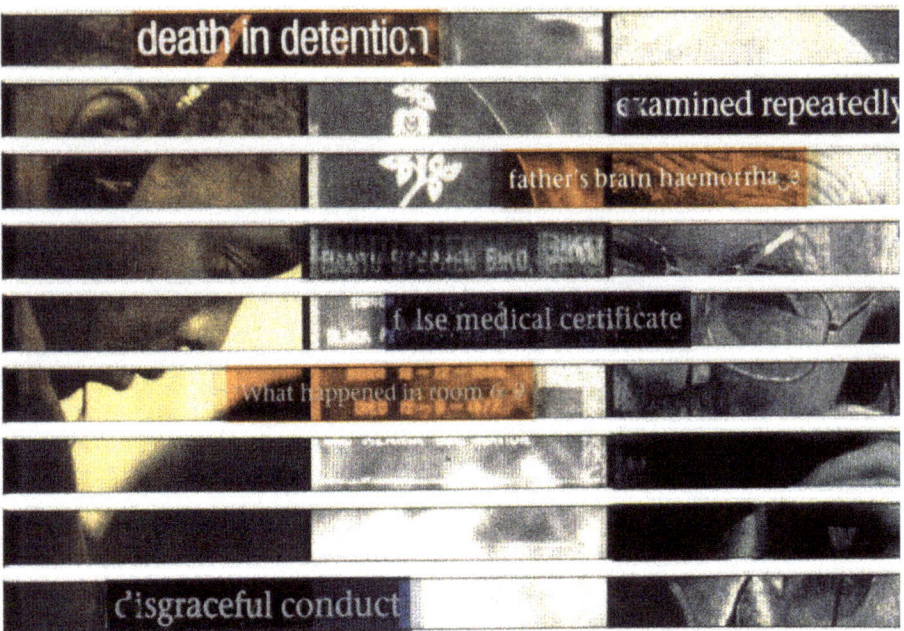

Figure 29   Sue Williamson, *Nkosinathi Biko – False medical certificate – Dr. Benjamin Tucker*

In my work, I try to recontextualize issues of contemporary South African history in such a way as to engage a wider public in the profound issues sometimes masked by media hype. By mediating through art, the information offered for public consumption in the mass media, I try to give dispassionate readings and offer new opportunities for engagement. Art can provide a distance and a space for such considerations.[82]

Paul Stopforth's portraits of the tormentors of his friend Steve Biko *The Interrogators* have been displayed in the National Gallery already during apartheid. Obviously, the regime did not take art particularly seriously as a medium of critique within its own borders. When the "protest art" however began to get exposure in the outside world, the authorities intervened. Stopforth was denied the participation in the Valparaiso Biennale in Chile 1981. The works submitted by the artist *Steve Biko* and *We Do*

---

[82] Sue Williamson, Looking Back, Looking Forward: An Overview of South African Art, in: *Liberated Voices. Contemporary Art from South Africa*, München et al., 1999, 33.

Guilt, Reconciliation and Grace 71

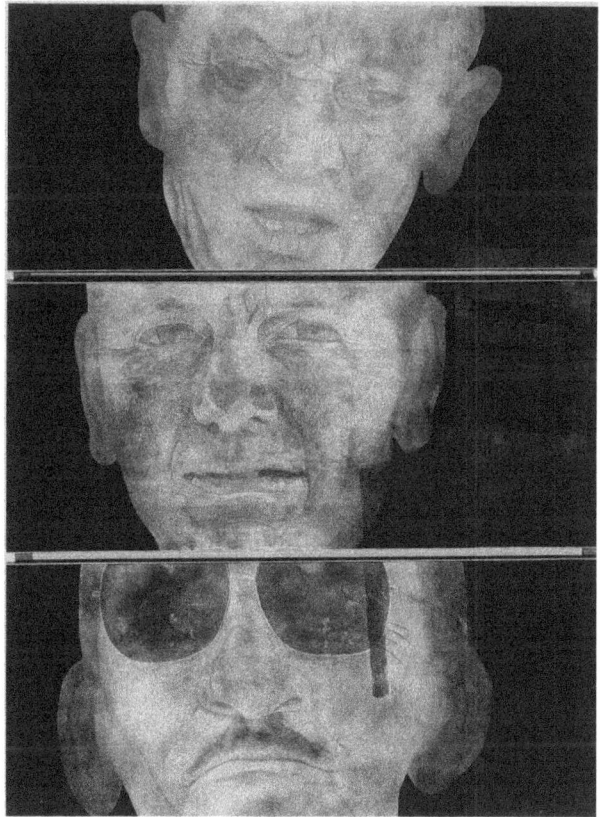

Figure 30   Paul Stopforth, *The Interrogators*

It, two graphite drawings of distorted hands and feet, were classified as political statements by the government officials in charge.[83]

The three portraits of Biko's tormentors, in cold grey, *The Interrogators* show in detail the faces of the secret police officers (Figure 30). Painted in front of a dark background they nearly fill the whole picture. Only perceptible in deep shadow is a chair that transgresses the three canvases and connects them to a triptych. Stopforth himself gives a hint for its interpretation:

> My purpose was to show how terribly ordinary these man looked – except perhaps the one with dark glasses (Colonel Harold Snyman).

---

[83] Cf. Williamson, Looking Back, 36f. and 32.

> The shadow of the chair is a reference to the "struggle" that was supposed to have taken place while Steve was in their custody.[84] The most mundane objects can take on frightening connotations in prison and interrogation spaces.[85]

A torture chair also plays a role in Hong Song-Dam's cycle *20 days in water*. It symbolizes being bound and at the mercy of the torturers. That at least one of them could be identified is due to two small pencil portraits, which Hong drew from memory.

In her much-acclaimed book *Country of my Skull* writer and journalist Antjie Krog has assembled testimonies in front of the TRC and interview sequences with participants in a loose manner, that throws particular light on the events around the TRC. This is interwoven with self-reflections of the white Afrikaaner woman that she is. The collage of voices that evolved out of this blurs the boundaries between journalism and literature. Krog knows how to illustrate the whole absurdity of the apartheid system in a short note about an excursion of the press corps to the prison Robben Island.

> On Tuesday the media sail out to Robben Island for a press conference. Despite the crowd of blistering pink tourists, one does not travel that distance by boat untouched. The cliché that is Table Mountain stands breathlessly in blue; the sea is quiet, glaucous heaving. And you think of the countless soul-destroying crossings made in this boat, the *Susan Kruger*. Named after the wife of Justice Minister Jimmy Kruger, himself enshrined in infamy for remarking that the death of Steve Biko left him cold.[86] As the boat slips out of the harbor, I think of Biko and how his story is the only famous one that has not been put before the Truth Commission. Because his family chose to take the Commission to the Constitutional court,

---

[84] According to the testimonies of the perpetrators Biko died accidentally, when they tried to force him to sit down.

[85] Quoted in Williamson, Looking Back, 42.

[86] Cf. also the movie *Goodbye Bafana* (2007) according to the notes of James Gregory (with Bob Graham), *Goodbye Bafana: Nelson Mandela, my prisoner, my friend*, London 1995, one of the wards of Nelson Mandela, that shows how the white racist ward and Mandela become closer. Anthony Sampson, *Mandela. The authorized Biography*, New York 1999, 217, voices criticism about the role of Gregory. In Nelson Mandela, *Long Walk to Freedom*, Boston 1994, 614–616 and 672, Gregory is mentioned in passing, not in a negative way.

we never got to hear about the last time they saw him, how they remember him, how his children are coping without him, even as they live in his gigantic shadow.[87]

The collage and patchwork technique that is applied by most of the writers and artists who have been introduced here is suitable for the fragmentary nature of the experiences that have to be coped with. Their work of preserving memories is fractured in many ways – a striving for truth.

2 Beyond Apocalypse – Dealing with guilt in societal transformation processes

There is a grave risk that after the overthrow of a dictatorship, or the end of a bloody civil war, there will be an overriding desire to suppress and forget the horror of what has been done as quickly as possible; most people just want to get on with their lives. How to define an epoch? – a question that was raised in the first chapter – returns here in ethical form: for the sake of a feigned new beginning the perpetrators get off lightly, while the victims are left alone with their trauma. Theologically, Johann Baptist Metz sees here a structural parallel in Christianity. The "soteriological circle" that has already been quoted leads to the constellation "that the church is more at ease with the guilty perpetrators than with the innocent victims."[88] This is countered by an aesthetic securing of evidence as has been demonstrated above in different domains. Metz's repeated polemic against an aesthetization of intellectual discourses including theology seems to me orientated towards the classical identification of aesthetics and beauty.[89] I apply however a much broader concept of aesthetics, that comprises the perception of ugly and evil as well as the suffering of the victims. The strenuous reconstruction of the relationship between aesthetics and ethics is not about an aesthetization of suffering in the sense of its glorification but about its disclosure, its treatment and the preservation of memory. This is theologically in line with Metz's program of *memoria passionis*, as has been shown repeatedly. At least five themes

---

[87] Krog, *Country*, 419f. Biko's family attended the hearings of the five perpetrators, who had applied to the amnesty committee. Yet they did not testify in front of the committee for gross human right violations but themselves pursued a lawsuit against the TRC.

[88] Metz, *Memoria*, 57; see above (p.56).

[89] Cf. op. cit., 18f., 105 und 138.

are addressed in this connection on a regular basis: The resistance against forgetting, the wish to understand what has happened, the expectation that the perpetrators show repentance, the question whether amnesty or mercy should be granted and the necessity to compensate the victims.

Tell the story, not withholding, suppressing or trying to forget as soon as possible

In spite of all the criticisms of the South African Truth and Reconciliation Commission, it is always acknowledged that it granted the victims a forum where they could get the horror they had experienced off their chests. The possibility of addressing someone, to have a vis-à-vis with someone who listens, is a first step toward healing memories. The names of the victims may not be forgotten and the names of the perpetrators may not be withheld. Even more, the perpetrators must be urged to confess their deeds – through which they themselves have been dehumanized as well.

Antjie Krog, Hwang Sok-Yong and Uwe Timm, in their writings, pluck personal fragments of contemporary history from the waters of forgetfulness and weave nets of memory that make repression impossible.[90] Gerhard Richter, Hong Song-Dam, Sue Williamson and Paul Stopforth enlarge this literary memory with a visual dimension. They are repeatedly reminiscent of the passion of Christ. The aesthetic landscapes of memory are at the same time attempts by the artists to reconstruct their own identity in view of their own role as a victim, or are driven by the wish to understand what has happened through the guilty involvement of their own families.

No understanding of the deed, but a desire to understand what has happened

Even more than forty years after the "German autumn" the names of most of those who fired fatal shots are not known. The surviving terrorists keep persistently silent, following the code of honor once constrained, that revealing the names would be treason. The relatives of the victims on the other hand finally want to know who has done it. It is eerie that the court exhibits from back then are analyzed with the latest forensic methods.

---

[90] This is also the strong point of the 9/11 memorial; see above (pp.19–22).

One of the most urgent goals of the South African Truth and Reconciliation Commission was therefore to reconstruct the terrible things that happened in the name of the apartheid regime, as well as its fiercest opponents.[91] Antjie Krog is suffering beneath the weight of the testimonials of the witnesses, shocked what her own people have done to the Black population. Uwe Timm is stunned by the normality of the horror that is reflected in the diary entries of his brother. Hwang Sok-Yong finally sends his protagonist, Ryu Yosop, on a journey into the past that reveals to him bit by bit the evil deeds his older brother Yohan was involved in. Hong Song-Dam, Paul Stopford and Sue Williamson give the perpetrators a face and bring their deeds into the visual domain. Repeatedly the wish is articulated: that the perpetrators show repentance.

Forgiveness demands repentance, only then does reconciliation become possible

A frequent argument in the public debate (2007/08) about amnesty for the RAF terrorists Brigitte Mohnhaupt and Christian Klar was that this was impossible, because they showed no sign of repentance for their deeds. Leading church representatives like the then chair of the EKD and bishop of Berlin-Brandenburg, Wolfgang Huber, also joined the discussion: "One would like to have certainty that Christian Klar repents his deeds." In a more sophisticated manner, the bishop of Hannover Margot Käßmann (in office 1999–2010) opined: "I wonder, if the perpetrators are big enough to confess their guilt [...] That must be bitter, but it is necessary if there should be ways into the future."

The perspective of the victims seems in contrast to be more realistic. Viveka Hillegaart, daughter of the attaché for economics, Dr. Heinz Hillegaart, who was killed during the hostage-taking in the German embassy in Stockholm, said in a conversation with Anne Siemens:

> I approved that the perpetrators were released from prison early in the 1990s. [...] I supported the high sentences for the perpetrators in 1977, murder deserves severe punishment. This is the only possibility for the constitutional state to demonstrate the limits to the perpetrator. But nearly two decades later it would not have made sense either to remain in the past and retain the sentence till the end. It was more important to advance towards a solution to the

---

[91] Cf. Krog, *Country*, 82 and 99f.

conflict. We never received a sign of repentance from the perpetrators, but I did not expect that either. Parts of their former thought patterns might still prevail in their heads today. Yet they have renounced their means. That is what counts. That they would not repeat their deeds in this form, is probably the only repentance they can demonstrate.[92]

Christa Baronin von Mirbach, wife of the defense attaché Andreas Baron von Mirbach, who was also killed in the Stockholm hostage-taking, goes even further in her statements:

After Andreas' death I had considered talking with the perpetrators in prison about their guilt. I certainly did not want to discuss with them what motivated their deeds. No, I wanted to introduce them to a possibility of how they could cope with their stricken conscience. They also had to be haunted by the terrifying images of their deeds, I thought. I wanted to tell them, that there is a God, who forgives guilt through Jesus Christ and provides the possibility of a new beginning. I know that Andreas would have agreed with this.[93]

Even if Christa von Mirbach has not followed up these considerations because of the media,[94] this demonstrates again that the initiatives come from the victims. It is even more nightmarish to read the reports about a therapeutic group of former members of the RAF and the *Bewegung 2. Juni*, which focus on the victimization of the perpetrators. Any thought of repentance or even reconciliation with the victims or their families still seems far away.[95]

As chair of the TRC Desmond Tutu has repeatedly pointed to the nearly incomprehensible will to forgiveness by the victims.

---

[92] Viveka Hillegaart quoted in: Siemens, *RAF*, 101f.; cf. Carolin Emcke, *Stumme Gewalt. Nachdenken über die RAF*, Frankfurt a.M. 2009.

[93] Christa von Mirbach quoted op. cit., 70.

[94] Ibid.

[95] Cf. *Nach dem bewaffneten Kampf. Ehemalige Mitglieder der RAF und Bewegung 2. Juni sprechen mit Therapeuten über ihre Vergangenheit*, Angelika Holderberg (ed.), Gießen 2007; Clais von Mirbach compares this strategy of suppression with the behavior of the Nazis after the end of their reign that has been castigated by the RAF (in: Siemens, *RAF*, 67). Jürgen Habermas early on talked about leftist fascism (*Linksfaschismus*) in this respect.

The most forgiving people I have ever come across are people who have suffered – it is as if suffering has ripped them open into empathy. I am talking about wounded healers.[96]

In contrast he bemoans how little repentance those who were responsible show for their deeds.[97] Antjie Krog expresses in her book several times her shame about this imbalance. Alan Boesak, like Tutu one of the pioneering voices of Black Theology,[98] criticizes the TRC fiercely, by talking of "an almost calculated kind of emotional blackmail":

If you did not forgive your torturer, you were made to feel as if there was something wrong with you. [...] There is a place for rightful anger. [...] So far, only forgiveness by the victims has been truly realized. All the other elements without which reconciliation cannot be genuine – restitution, reparation, restoration, justice – are left to languish on the ash heap of the stories, told, listened to, not acted upon, and forgotten.[99]

Tutu argues in contrast: "If the victim could forgive only when the culprit confessed, then the victim would be locked into the culprit's whim, locked into victimhood, whatever her own attitude or intention."[100] This is a view that is affirmed by testimonies of the aggrieved parties. Therefore, it makes sense to speak about self-reconciliation or self-acceptance, as it is paradigmatically expressed in the slogan "Black is beautiful." With recourse to the works of Sigmund Freud the psychoanalyst Frantz Fanon, one of the fathers of postcolonial critique, argued that the victims have internalized the perspective of the oppressors.[101] This heteronomy

---

[96] Tutu quoted in Krog, *Country*, 24.

[97] Cf. op. cit., 239.

[98] Cf. Allan A. Boesak, *The Tenderness of Conscience. African Renaissance and the Spirituality of Politics*, Stellenbosch 2005, 173, 175, 185 and 195ff; Tutu, *No future*, 58, 138, 184–189 and 220.

[99] Boesak, *Tenderness*, 195–198.

[100] Tutu, *No future*, 220.

[101] Cf. Frantz Fanon, *Black Skin, White Masks*, New York 1994 [frz. 1952]; id., *The Wretched of the Earth*, New York 2005 [frz. 1961].

in self-perception has to be overcome in the self-acceptance of reconciliation with one self.[102]

In South Korea the former representatives of the military government and their henchmen so far also have shown little repentance. The societal refurbishment still lies ahead. President Park Geun-Hye, the daughter of dictator Park Chung-Hee, surprisingly came to power in democratic elections (2013–2017), and with her the old corrupt power elites. Her career came to a disreputable end through an impeachment, called for by peaceful candlelight demonstrations by the people, and finally unanimously supported by the constitutional court. Similar to South Africa, the young South Korean democracy also has to stand the test. Even if the impeachment and the subsequent trial as well as the conviction have demonstrated that the independent jurisdiction is functioning, till the end there were also manifestations of sympathy for Park especially among the elderly.

The Christian churches were also divided. An ambivalent role was played, for example, by the prominent regime critic Reverend In Myong-Jin (*1946) who, in December 2016, accepted the election as interim chairman of the failing government party. Also Kim Chi-Ha, who had been sentenced to death by the father, Park Chung-Hee, all of a sudden showed sympathy for his daughter. On the other hand, Kim's longtime friend and political companion Hong Song-Dam, in his well-known radical manner, took a stance against Park Geun-Hye with biting caricatures. All three contexts are affected by a complicated mixture of interests regarding the societal processes of reconciliation.

To grant amnesty or mercy

While amnesty – for example on the occasion of a far-reaching change of regime – has to be regulated by law, mercy can be granted by a political office holder, usually the head of state. Desmond Tutu emphasized with regard to the South African TRC, that this is about "amnesty not amnesia." This is well-founded in the choice of a third way beyond tribunal or general pardon. Resist oblivion! – Here closes the circle of our argument.

---

[102] This has also been emphazised early on by Allan A. Boesak, *Farewell to Innocence. A Socio-Ethical Study on Black Theology and Power*, Maryknoll, NY 1977, 92f. Cf. James Cone, *Black Theology and Black Power*, New York 1969, 19f. For Latin America Paulo Freire, *Pedagogy of the Oppressed*, New York etc. 2000 [1970; Port. 1968] and his concept of "conscientization."

Only those who were willing to confess their deeds in front of the commission would be allowed to apply for amnesty.

The mercy granted individually is not bound by any precondition in the end.[103] Thereby neither the deed is relativized nor an existing conviction abolished.

> An appeal to mercy does not extinguish the judgment. This judgment remains in effect. Only its enforcement is terminated – out of mercy. The decision has only to be concerned about the human being. Other reasons don't have to be named. [...] Only the right to reprieve makes our law human. Behind it the knowledge about God's grace emerges. His contemporaries said about Jesus that he speaks "words of grace". His cross is the sign of grace. Therefore, it is the decisive Christian symbol. Without grace our world would be desolate. Our law would be also desolate, if the possibility of mercy would not exist.[104]

In this regard one always has to keep in mind Metz's admonition of the "soteriological circle." Human bestowal of mercy is only possible in memory of the victims, who are salvaged in the *memoria passionis* in God.

Reparations for the victims here and now

The question of possible reparations for the victims has been hardly thought through theologically. With regard to the general socio-economic conditions there exists a clear difference between the situations in Germany – and to a lesser degree South Korea – and South Africa. Apart from the principal question, how the loss of human lives or the pain endured can be converted into money, in most countries in the Global South social security systems are nonexistent and the state is financially too weak to compensate for the victims. Yet the loss of a husband or father for instance has concrete existential consequences for the prospects of the bereaved. One of the repeated criticisms on the South African TRC

---

[103] Cf. Desmond Tutu, *No Future Without Forgiveness*, London etc. 1999, 48.

[104] Wolfgang Huber, Christian Klar: Recht und Gnade, Kolumne in *Bild* vom 2.02.2007, www.ekd.de on 24.03.07; cf. id., *Gerechtigkeit und Recht. Grundlinien christlicher Rechtsethik*, Gütersloh 1996, 359–361.

therefore was that it did not succeed in compensating the victims at least materially.

First of all, it applies generally, that this cannot be an act of compassion, but that the victims have well-nigh a right on compensation. Theologically speaking God himself grants them justice. The *option for the poor* propagated originally by Latin American liberation theology might return here in a new shape. A further point of contact are Jesus' healings and feedings that symbolize the coming of the kingdom of God in the here and now. As "handsel for the Kingdom of Heaven" they relieve the material need of the poor and oppressed, without abolishing the tension between the "already now" and the "not yet".

3 In conflict with God

That God should be the one who can unconditionally grant grace to the perpetrators is met by many victims with disbelief. Already in the secular sphere such unconditional reprieve then granted by state authority provokes lack of understanding. Corinna Ponto, daughter of Jürgen Ponto, chairman of the board of the Dresdner Bank, who was murdered by the RAF in 1977 complains about the privilege of the terrorists to be able to become "ex-perpetrators":

> Who became a victim once can never become an ex-victim. Yet the perpetrators are frequently referred to as "former" terrorists today. This "ex" is a privilege. I am not aware of an ex-murderer, or an ex-child kidnapper. All those however who were RAF members and live in our society again today call themselves ex-terrorists. [...] Mercy as such is an elementary theme and a good thing, but not against the setting of insincerity. I personally have never been reached by an honest, exciting, distinguished distanciation.[105]

The desire for just punishment does not exclude categorically the possibility of mercy, only the perpetrators should show clearly their remorse. The gospel of Luke illustrates this perfectly with the story of the two criminals, who are crucified together with Jesus. One of them mocks him even in the face of death, the other shows repentance: "We are punished justly, for we are getting what our deeds deserve" (Lk 23,41a). He

---

[105] Corinna Ponto, in: Siemens, *RAF*, 119f.

is promised paradise by Jesus. In medieval art the soul of the converted criminal is depicted as a small human being that leaves the body to be received by angels. The soul of the remorseless one is awaited by a creature from hell.[106] God's judgment "will confront each human being with his or her own life story."[107]

> What kind of end of the world and its history it would be, if violence and injustice on the earth would remain covered in the darkness of the past; when its completion could be reached defying the suffering and the tears of the innocent. Loyalty with the *victim* means, to name the injustice that he or she had to endure. Loyalty with the *perpetrator* means, to take him or her seriously as well, and that happens by setting the atrocities "in the light of your presence" (Ps 90,8). Because God's goal with creation, the establishment of justice and peace (*Shalom*), remains tied to this loyalty, therefore the path to completion leads through judgment.[108]

Elsa Tamez (b. 1951), a Mexican theologian, who taught in Costa Rica until her retirement, declares the victims, the poor and oppressed themselves, the subjects of forgiveness, by referring to Jon Sobrino:

> if the poor are the ones offended, the possibility of others' sharing in the forgiveness they have received from God will have to be mediated by them. The honest human being who recognizes his or her own sin in the presence of those who are excluded will feel freed from guilt when he or she has been forgiven by God through them. The importance of recognizing in the poor those who can forgive is that one's own sin against them can be acknowledged.[109]

---

[106] Cf. Aloys Butzkamm, *Christliche Ikonographie. Zum Verstehen mittelalterlicher Kunst*, Paderborn 1996, 84–87 using the example of a crucifixion image from the collection of the museum Unterlinden in Colmar.

[107] Dietrich and Link, *Die dunklen Seiten Gottes, vol. 2, Allmacht und Ohnmacht*, 319.

[108] Ibid.

[109] Elsa Tamez, *The Amnesty of Grace. Justification by Faith from a Latin American Perspective*, Nashville 1993, 163f. Cf. Dietrich and Link, *Die dunklen Seiten Gottes 2*, 356–359.

The last question however, whether there is eternal condemnation for those who do not show repentance, or whether God's will to be gracious includes them in the end, remains controversial in theology.

> Is it definite that the evildoers go to "hell"? If this is what it comes down to, then the dividing and distinguishing light of justice in the end only would petrify the contradictions of the earth. It would have confirmed the darkness forever. Is that imaginable? Or may we hope for *more* regarding the end? Hope, that this light is even superior to the last darkness, that it will assert life also "in darkness and shadow of death" and lead it to victory, that God does not capitulate in front of this final goal of creation?[110]

The perpetrators and their sympathizers have developed different strategies to relate themselves to God. During the military dictatorship the conservative protestant churches in South Korea turned against Minjung theology with the argument that the church should not mingle with politics, but concentrate fully on God, while many of their representatives could hardly hide their sympathies for those in power. The South African apartheid regime openly claimed to have God on its side. The "state theology" denounced by the kairos document was supported by white churches like the Dutch Reformed Church.[111] A third option beside supposed separation or inclusion is the revaluation of all values, as it was carried out by Gudrun Enslin, the daughter of a protestant minister. Stefan Aust reports, how she proclaimed her "bad religion" during an excessive LSD night in Berlin. In her reformulations of the Ten Commandments for example the commandment "you have to kill" stood central. Characteristics of this "fundamentalist religion of self-redemption of protestant brand" are poverty and illegality of its followers, a dualism, that articulates itself in a strict thinking in terms of friend or foe, and the "primacy of practice" or the "propaganda of the deed."[112]

If the perpetrators obviously have a distorted relationship with God and are depending on God's grace and the will of the victims to reconciliation,

---

[110] Dietrich and Link, *Die dunklen Seiten Gottes* 2, 357.

[111] Cf. *Christen im Widerstand. Die Diskussion um das südafrikanische KAIROS Dokument*, Stuttgart 1987, 19.

[112] Cf. Aust, *Baader-Meinhof-Komplex*, 107; Herrmann, "Unsere Söhne und Töchter"; id., Ulrike Meinhof und Gudrun Enslin – Vom Protestantismus zum Terrorismus, in: *Zur Vorstellung des Terrors: Die RAF-Ausstellung*, vol. 2, Göttingen 2005, 112–114.

what rests for the latter ones? Biblical texts like the psalms (Ps 7,9f; Ps 10; Ps 22,2f etc.) point the victims to the path of lamentation before God. Even to charge God seems to be possible. Job (23,1–7) wants to open a legal case with God. This problem has found its classical expression in theodicy. How can God allow suffering? In our concrete case also, how can God put the perpetrators in a better position than the victims? These charges are opposite to the oft-quoted willingness of the victims to reconciliation. They imitate in a certain sense God's graceful acts. The perpetrators on the other hand think that they have God at their disposal, and see themselves often as the ones who enforce God's judgment. For this arrogant blasphemy they will have to justify themselves in front of this very Judge. God encounters the victims in *compassion*. In Jesus Christ God himself trod the path of suffering. The thesis advocated by Jürgen Moltmann, that the crucifixion event has to be understood as a suffering *in* God in the end,[113] is countered by his fellow traveler in the new political theology Johann Baptist Metz, with the suffering *about* God.[114] These two possibilities to respond to theodicy can however be regarded as complementary. Not without ambivalence we cry out like the crucified on Golgotha (Mk 15,34) our suffering *about* God, hoping that God is present *in* this very suffering and we might be heard. Faith in a just and compassionate God has to endure this tension.

---

[113] Cf. Jürgen Moltmann, *Der gekreuzigte Gott. Das Kreuz Christi als Grund und Kritik christlicher Theologie*, München 1972.

[114] Cf. Metz, *Memoria Passionis*, 18.

Epilogue

On the tide of secularization, the face of God has been concealed in western culture. At the same time, the latter often denies its origins in Christian religion and iconography today. Theologians therefore have to uncover strenuously traces of God in contemporary culture. The two preceding chapters are an attempt to perform the necessary *aesthetic turn*.

Late modern hermeneutics locates the viewer in the picture. A Christian viewer can thus interpret a secular painting from the perspective of his or her religious convictions. It may however not be monopolized for Christian ends. The respect for the autonomy of the work of art requires the necessary distance. That includes the recognition of the right of people with other religious affiliations to interpret the painting in their own way. To give an example: the monochrome blue of a painting by Yves Klein will remind a Christian viewer of the color of heaven, while a Zen Buddhist might view the same picture and be reminded of "absolute nothingness."[1] A good work of art will never be exhausted by one interpretation, but produces in interaction with its viewers a plentitude of meanings. Yet, it sets the limits of its interpretation by itself, it does not allow just anything to be done with it.

As we have observed, on looking closer, many iconographical motives still stem from Christian tradition. The generative themes of life are another bridge between art and religion, for which Christian faith – as well as other religions – offers a reservoir of stories and generative themes to deal with them. Not only in times of joy, but also in times of suffering and failure.

In Christianity the presence of God in human suffering and the defeat of death through the resurrection of Jesus Christ have proven to be powerful stories in situations of oppression and suffering. In Korea it was the Minjung theologians in the 1970s and 1980s who encountered – in the suffering *minjung*, the poor, workers and farmers – the suffering Christ. This made them the avant-garde of social change. In parallel, South African black theology saw in him the black messiah, who carried out a re-evaluation of the discrimination because of skin color superimposed by the white minority: "Black is beautiful." Germany does not have a comparable liberation theology movement. Yet the mainstream churches

---

[1] In Christian–Buddhist dialogue one also talks about the "god filled gap" in this respect.

have at least identified the overcoming of poverty and oppression in the Global South as a field of their diaconic work. Further, there are overlaps between church initiatives like the *Kirchentag* and parts of the peace and ecology movement. There are however only a few theologians, mainly from the background of new political theology and feminist theology, who have addressed the challenges of their context theologically.

In the events of 9/11 the risks and repercussions of globalization have been symbolically condensed. Neither the art world nor contextual theologies have been left unaffected, but have been challenged to reformulate their agendas. While artists have responded to these transformation processes in many ways – often by making use of Christian patterns of interpretation, sometimes also those of different religious origin – theology remains awkwardly silent.

The positions of Karlheinz Stockhausen and Adam Small mark the range of the aesthetic discourse on violence and reconciliation. I have countered Stockhausen's ethical indifference with the three criteria of *vision*, *distance* and *unscathedness*. Adam Small on the other hand seems to show how artists and theologians can enter into a dialogue that is fruitful for both sides. Because of that an *interstitial space* or *Third Space* is opened up, in which one can negotiate between art and theology.[2] Artists tackle the generative themes of life in an aesthetic way. With their works of art, they create an interpretative space that allows multiple readings. Theologians are hermeneuticians of life, who interweave (*versprechen*; Ernst Lange) biblical stories and the generative themes that guide them with the human life stories and the particular generative themes that inform them in a creative process. Theological/religious language can serve to illuminate secular circumstances; at the same time, in the secular language of art, theological content might emerge. Artists in a way then become theologians and theologians become artists.

---

[2] See above (p.1f. and p.31f.). Cf. Volker Küster, Who, with whom, about what? Exploring the Landscape of Inter-religious Dialogue, in: *Exchange* 33, 2004, 73–92. https://doi.org/10.1163/1572543041172666

Bibliography

Aust, Stefan and Schnibben, Cordt, *11. September. Geschichte eines Terrorangriffs*, Stuttgart etc. 2002.

Aust, Stefan, *Der Baader Meinhof Komplex*, Hamburg 1986.

Beck, Ulrich, *Was ist Globalisierung?*, Frankfurt a.M. 1997.

Biko, Steve, *I Write What I Like*, Johannesburg 2004 [London 1978].

Boesak, Allan A., *Farewell to Innocence. A Socio-Ethical Study on Black Theology and Power*, Maryknoll, NY 1977.

——, *The Tenderness of Conscience. African Renaissance and the Spirituality of Politics*, Stellenbosch 2005.

Boff, Leonardo, *Der dreieinige Gott*, Düsseldorf 1987.

Bonhoeffer, Dietrich, *Ethik*, München 1992.

Borgman, Eric, *Metamorfosen. Over religie en moderne cultuur*, Kampen 2006.

Buruma, Ian and Margalit, Avishai, *Occidentalism. A Short History of Anti-Westernism*, London 2004.

Butzkamm, Aloys, *Christliche Ikonographie. Zum Verstehen mittelalterlicher Kunst*, Paderborn 1996.

Chung-Hee, Lim and Jung, Andreas (eds.), *Malttugi. Texte und Bilder aus der Minjung Kulturbewegung in Südkorea*, Heidelberg 1986.

Cone, James, *Black Theology and Black Power*, New York 1969.

de Gruchy, John W., *Christianity, Art and Transformation. Theological Aesthetics in the Struggle for Justice*, Cambridge, New York 2001.

——, *Reconciliation. Restoring Justice*, Minneapolis 2002.

Der Schock des 11. September und das Geheimnis des Anderen. Eine Dokumentation, Berlin 2002.

Devereux, Mary, Beauty and evil: The case of Leni Riefenstahl's *Triumph of the Will*, in: *Aesthetics and Ethics. Essays at the Intersection*, Jerrold Levinson (ed.), Cambridge 1998, 227–256.

Dienstag 11. September 2001, Reinbek bei Hamburg 2001.

Dietrich, Walter and Link, Christian, *Die Dunklen Seiten Gottes*, 2 Vols., Neukirchen-Vluyn 1997 and 2000.

Documenta 12 Kassel 16/06–23/09, 2007. Katalog, Köln 2007.

Documenta11_Plattform5: Ausstellung, Katalog, Ostfildern-Ruit 2002.

Documenta11_Plattform5: Ausstellung, Kurzführer, Ostfildern-Ruit 2002.

Documenta11_Plattform5: Ausstellungsorte, Ostfildern-Ruit 2002.

Dube, Musa W., *Postcolonial Feminist Interpretation of the Bible*, St. Louis, Missouri 2000.

Elger, Dietmar, *Gerhard Richter, Maler*, Köln 2002.

Enwezor, Okwui, *The Short Century. Independence and Liberation Movements in Africa 1945–1994*, München etc. 2001.

Erbele-Küster, Dorothea, Ungerechte Texte und gerechte Sprache. Überlegungen zur Hermeneutik des Bibelübersetzens, in: *Die Bibel – übersetzt in gerechter Sprache? Grundlagen einer neuen Übersetzung*, Gütersloh 2005, 222–234.

Fanon, Frantz, *Black Skin, White Masks*, New York 1994 [frz. 1952].

——, *The Wretched of the Earth*, New York 2005 [frz. 1961].

Frettlöh, Magdalene L., "Der Mensch heißt Mensch, weil er ... vergibt"? Philosophisch-politische und anthropologische Vergebungsdiskurse im Licht der fünften Vaterunserbitte, in: *"Wie? Auch wir vergeben unseren Schuldigern?"*, Jabboq 5, Jürgen Ebach et al. (eds.), Gütersloh 2004, 179–215.

Friedel, Helmut, *Gerhard Richter. Birkenau*, Köln 2016.

Fukuyama, Francis, *End of History and the Last Man*, New York 1992.

Grabowski, Klaus H., Die Stimmen der Intellektuellen und ihr Echo, in: Felicitas von Aretin and Bernd Wannenmacher (eds.), Weltlage. *Der 11. September, die Politik und die Kulturen*, Opladen 2002, 195–208.

Graf, Friedrich Wilhelm, *Die Wiederkehr der Götter. Religion in der modernen Kultur*, München 2004.

——, *Götter global. Wie die Welt zum Supermarkt der Religionen wird*, München 2014.

Gregory, James (with Bob Graham), *Goodbye Bafana: Nelson Mandela, my prisoner, my friend*, London 1995.

Griffith, Lee, *The War on Terrorism and the Terror of God*, Grand Rapids 2002.

Hardt, Michael and Negri, Antonio, *Empire*, Cambridge 2000.

Hermann, Jörg, "Unsere Söhne und Töchter" Protestantismus und RAF-Terrorismus in den 1970er Jahren, in: Kraushaar, *RAF*, Vol. 1, 644–656.

——, Ulrike Meinhof und Gudrun Enslin – Vom Protestantismus zum Terrorismus, in: *Zur Vorstellung des Terrors: Die RAF-Ausstellung*, Vol. 2, Göttingen 2005, 112–114.

Hirschler, Horst, Wo war Gott am 11. September?, in: *Zeitzeichen* 2, 11/2001, 14–17.

Holderberg, Angelika, *Nach dem bewaffneten Kampf. Ehemalige Mitglieder der RAF und Bewegung 2. Juni sprechen mit Therapeuten über ihre Vergangenheit*, Gießen 2007.

Hong, Sung-Dam, Resistance and Meditation in: *EAST Wind*, New York 2003.

Horn, Rebecca, *Bodylandscapes. Zeichnungen, Skulpturen, Installationen 1964–2004*, German guide to the exhibition in the art collection of Nordrhein-Westfalen from 2 October, 2004 to 1 January, 2005.

Huber, Wolfgang, *Gerechtigkeit und Recht. Grundlinien christlicher Rechtsethik*, Gütersloh 1996.

Huntington, Samuel P., *Clash of Civilisations and the Remaking of World Order*, New York 1996.

Hwang, Sok-Yong, *Der ferne Garten*, München 2005.

——, *Der Gast*, München 2007.

——, *Die Geschichte des Herrn Han*, München 2005 [Kor. 1972].

Im Blickfeld: Gerhard Richter in der Hamburger Kunsthalle, with a text by Uwe Schneede, Hamburg 2006.

Jeanrond, Werner, Thinking about God Today, in: Werner G. Jeanrond and Aasulf Lande (eds.), *The Concept of God in Global Dialogue*, Maryknoll, New York 2005, 89–97.

Jihad Against Jews and Crusaders. World Islamic Front Statement, https://fas.org/irp/world/para/docs/980223-fatwa.htm on 05.08.2020.

Kermani, Navid, Die Gärten der Märtyrer, in: *Religion und Terror*, 63–75.

Kim, Sung-Soo, Die Tonghak-Bewegung in Korea. Sozio-ökonomische Hintergründe und ideologischer Wandlungsprozeß, Dissertation, Frankfurt a.M. 1980.

Kim, Yong Choon, *The Ch'ondogyo Concept of Man. An Essence of Korean Thought*, Seoul 1978.

Kraushaar, Wolfgang (ed.), *Die RAF und der linke Terrorismus*, 2 Vols., Hamburg 2006.

Krog, Antjie, *Country of my Skull*, London 1999.

Küenzlen, Gottfried, Nach dem 11. September: Fundamentalismus – Phantom oder Phänomen?, in: Hubertus Lutterbach and Jürgen Manemann (eds.), *Religion und Terror. Stimmen zum 11. September aus Christentum, Islam und Judentum*, Münster 2002, 78–93.

Kürschner, Frank und Hinz, Rudolf, *Christen im Widerstand. Die Diskussion um das südafrikanische KAIROS Dokument*, Stuttgart 1987.

Küster, Volker, *A Protestant Theology of Passion. Minjung Theology revisited*, Leiden 2010.

——, Indebted to Kinship – The Project of an "Abrahamic ecumene" Contested, in: id. and Gé Speelman (eds.), *Islam in the Netherlands. Between Religious Studies and Interreligious Dialogue*, Münster 2010, 163–180.

——, *Jesus und das Volk im Markusevangelium. Ein Beitrag zum interkulturellen Gespräch in der Exegese*, Neukirchen-Vluyn 1996.

—, *The Many Faces of Jesus Christ. Intercultural Christology*, Maryknoll, NY 2001.

—, *Theologie im Kontext. Zugleich ein Versuch über die Minjung-Theologie*, Nettetal 1995.

—, Von der lokalen Theologie zur neuen Katholizität. Robert J. Schreiters Suche nach einer Theologie zwischen dem Lokalen und dem Globalen, in: *Evangelische Theologie* 63, 2003, 362–374. https://doi.org/10.14315/evth-2003-0506

—, Who, with whom, about what? Exploring the Landscape of Interreligious Dialogue, in: *Exchange* 33, 2004, 73–92. https://doi.org/10.1163/1572543041172666

Link, Christian, Das Bilderverbot als Kriterium theologischen Redens von Gott, in: id., *Die Spur des Namens. Wege zur Erkenntnis Gottes und zur Erfahrung der Schöpfung. Theologische Studien*, Neukirchen-Vluyn 1997, 3–35.

—, Gott ist ein Fremdling, in: *Zeitzeichen* 3, 6/2002, 26–29.

Lutterbach, Hubertus and Manemann, Jürgen (eds.), *Religion und Terror. Stimmen zum 11. September aus Christentum, Islam und Judentum*, Münster 2002, 78–93.

Mackert, Gabriele et al. (eds.), *Attack. Kunst und Krieg in den Zeiten der Medien*, Katalog zur Ausstellung der Kunsthalle Wien 23 May to 21 September, 2003, Vienna 2003.

Made in Germany. Kurzführer / Short Guide, Hannover 2007.

Maluleke, Tinyiko, Of Collapsible Coffins and Ways of Dying. The Search for a Catholic Contextuality in African Perspective, in: *The Ecumenical Review* 54, 2002, 313–332. https://doi.org/10.1111/j.1758-6623.2002.tb00156.x

Mandela, Nelson, *Long Walk to Freedom*, Boston 1994.

Martig, Charles, Widerstand gegen den Bilderkrieg, in: *Zeitzeichen* 2, 11/2001, 52–54.

Martin Hielscher, *Uwe Timm*, München 2007.

Metz, Johann Baptist, *Memoria Passionis. Ein provozierendes Gedächtnis in pluralistischer Gesellschaft*, Freiburg etc. 2006.

Moltmann, Jürgen, *Gott in der Schöpfung. Ökologische Schöpfungslehre*, München 1987.

—, Das Ende als Anfang, in: *Zeitzeichen* 2, 12/2001, 40–43.

—, *Der gekreuzigte Gott. Das Kreuz Christi als Grund und Kritik christlicher Theologie*, München 1972.

—, *Trinität und Reich Gottes. Zur Gotteslehre*, München 1980.

Moore, Michael, *Fahrenheit 9/11* (2004).

Morrison, Toni, Die Toten des 11. September, in: *Dienstag 11. September*, 11–12.

Müller, Harald, *Das Zusammenleben der Kulturen. Ein Gegenentwurf zu Huntington*, Frankfurt a.M. 1998.

Nirumand, Bahmãn, *Persien, Modell eines Entwicklungslandes oder Die Diktatur der Freien Welt*, Hamburg 1967.

Panikkar, Raimon, *Gott, Mensch und Welt. Die Drei-Einheit der Wirklichkeit*, Petersberg 1999.

Paulo Freire, *Pedagogy of the Oppressed,* New York etc. 2000 [1970; Port. 1968].

Phyllis Trible and Letty M. Russel (eds.), *Hagar, Sarah and their Children. Jewish, Christian and Muslim Perspectives*, Louisville, Kentucky 2006.

Prints of Hong Seong-Dam, Seoul 1990.

Pui-Lan, Kwok et al. (eds.), *Empire and the Christian Tradition. New Readings of Classical Theologians*, Minneapolis 2007.

Robertson, Roland, Glocalization: Time – Space and Homogenity – Heterogenity, in: Scott Lash and Roland Robertson (eds.), *Global Modernities*, London 1995, 25–44.

Rosiny, Stephan, Der jihad im Islam, ein kontroverses Rechtsgutachten von 1998 und die Anschläge vom 11. September, in: *Weltlage*, 75–89. https://doi.org/10.1007/978-3-322-95043-7_5

Sahi, Joti, Terrorism and the clash of Civilisations on http://www.asianchristianart.org/news/ article6.htm on 3.09.2006.

Said, Edward W., *Culture and Imperialism*, London 1993.

Sampson, Anthony, *Mandela. The authorized Biography*, New York 1999.

Schreiber, Jürgen, *Ein Maler aus Deutschland. Gerhard Richter. Das Drama einer Familie*, Berlin 2007.

Schreiter, Robert J., *The New Catholicity. Theology between the Global and the Local*, Maryknoll, NY 1997.

Schwerfel, Heinz Peter (ed.), *Kunst nach Ground Zero*, Köln 2002.

Seel, Martin, *Ästhetik des Erscheinens*, Frankfurt a.M. 2003.

Shirin Neshat, Ausstellungskatalog Aarhus Kunstmuseum 2002.

Siemens, Anne, *Für die RAF war er das System, für mich der Vater. Die andere Geschichte des deutschen Terrorismus*, München 2007.

Sontag, Susan, Der Irrtum der Ausnahme, in: *Der Schock des 11. September und das Geheimnis des Anderen. Eine Dokumentation*, Berlin 2002, 40–42.

——, Feige waren die Mörder nicht, in: *Dienstag 11. September 2001*, Reinbek bei Hamburg 2001, 33–35.

——, *Regarding the Pain of Others*, London etc. 2003.

Soo-Il, Chai, Die Überwindung der Gewalt aus der Sicht der Opfer – Das Beispiel von Hong Sung Dam, in: Benjamin Simon and Henning Wrogemann (eds.), *Konviviale Theologie*, Festgabe für Theo Sundermeier zum 70. Geburtstag, Frankfurt a.M. 2005, 287–298.

Storr, Robert, *Gerhard Richter October 18, 1977*, New York 2000

——, *September. A History Painting by Gerhard Richter*, London 2009.

Sugirtharajah, R.S., *Postcolonial Reconfigurations. An Alternative Way of Reading the Bible and Doing Theology*, St. Louis 2003.

Tamez, Elsa, *The Amnesty of Grace. Justification by Faith from a Latin American Perspective*, Nashville 1993.

Timm, Uwe, *Am Beispiel meines Bruders*, München 2005.

——, *Der Freund und der Fremde*, München 2007.

——, *Heißer Sommer*, München 2007 [1974].

——, *Morenga*, München 1978.

——, *Rot*, München 2006 [2001].

Trible, Phyllis, *Texts of Terror. Literary-Feminist Readings of Biblical Narratives*, Philadelphia 1984.

Tutu, Desmond, *No Future Without Forgiveness*, London etc. 1999.

Unerwünschte Bilder. Hong, Sung-Dam. Holz und Linolschnitte aus Südkorea, ed. by Evangelische Erwachsenenbildung Niedersachsen, Göttingen 1990.

Villa-Vincencio, Charles and Verwoerd, Wilhelm (eds.), *Looking Back Reaching Forward. Reflections on the Truth and Reconciliation Commission of South Africa*, London and New York 2000.

Virilio, Paul, Vom Terror zur Apokalypse, in: *Der Schock des 11. September*, 44–53.

von Aretin, Felicitas and Wannenmacher, Bernd (eds.), Weltlage. *Der 11. September, die Politik und die Kulturen*, Opladen 2002.

Walther, Rudolf, Terror und Terrorismus. Eine begriffs- und sozialgeschichtliche Skizze, in: Wolfgang Kraushaar (ed.), *Die RAF und der linke Terrorismus*, Vol. 1, Hamburg 2006, 64–77.

Weems, Benjamin B., *Reforms, Rebellion and the Heavenly Way*, Tucson, Arizona 1964.

Weiermair, Peter, Überlegungen zum Thema Blut in der zeitgenössischen Kunst, in: *Blut. Kunst, Macht, Politik, Pathologie*, James M. Bradburne (ed.), München etc. 2001, 205–217.

Welten, Ruud, *Zinvol Geweld. Satre, Camus en Merlau-Ponty over terreur en terrorisme*, Kampen 2006.

Williamson, Sue, Looking Back, Looking Forward: An Overview of South African Art, in: *Liberated Voices. Contemporary Art from South Africa*, München etc. 1999.

Won-Cha, Ok Soong, *Der Einfluß der Donghak-Bewegung auf die Ausbildung der Minjung-Theologie in Korea*, Dissertation, Frankfurt a.M. 1986.

Wüstenberg, Ralf K., *The Political Dimension of Reconciliation. A Theological Analysis of Ways of Dealing with Guilt during the Transitions to Democracy in South Africa and Germany*, Grand Rapids and Cambridge 2009.

Zijlstra, Onno, *Ethiek en Esthetiek zijn Eén. Over Wittgensteins Tractatus 6.421*, Kamper Cahiers 69, Kampen 1990.

Index

aesthetic(s), 1, 2, 5, 14,16, 24, 31, 32, 35, 44, 47, 67, 68, 73, 74, 85, 86, 87
Ahn, Byung-Mu, 26
Albertz, Heinrich, 46
amnesty, 3, 34, 69, 73, 74, 75, 78, 79, 81, 92
apartheid, 65, 68, 69, 70, 72, 75
apocalypse, 3, 6, 22, 24, 73
Arad, Michael, 19, 20, 21
attack, 6, 7, 8, 9, 11, 12, 16, 18, 22, 23, 24, 90
Auschwitz, 26, 46
Aust, Stefan, 11, 44, 45, 46, 82, 85
Baader, Andreas, 46, 49
Baader-Meinhof, 3, 44, 45, 47, 48, 52, 55, 82, 87
Barns, Larry, 17
beauty, 1, 16, 73, 87
Beck, Ulrich, 24, 87
Biko, Nkosinathi 69, 70
Biko, Stephen, 69
Bin Laden, Osama, 7, 9, 10, 21
Blair, Tony, 22
Boesak, Alan A., 77, 78, 87
Boff, Leonardo, 27, 87
Bonhoeffer, Dietrich, 42, 87
Borgman, Eric, 27, 87
Bradburne, James M., 16, 92
Brus, Günter, 16
Buruma, Ian, 9, 8
Bush, George W., 10, 26
Butzkamm, Aloys, 81, 87
capitalism, 3, 24, 26, 28
Chicane, Frank, 68
Christology, 2, 90
Chun, Tae-Il, 67
Chun, Doo-Hwan, 43
Cold War, 11
colonialism; colonization, 33, 39, 43, 45, 51; 9

communism; communist, 10; 21, 33, 35, 43, 65, 67
compassion, 4, 40, 83
Cone, James, 78, 87
conflict, 2, 3, 5, 6, 16, 25, 29, 31, 41, 43, 76, 80
courage, 6, 9, 10, 13, 41, 46
criterion; criteria, 1, 16, 69; 3, 5, 17, 86
cross; crucifixion, 26, 28, 49, 55, 56, 68, 79; 80, 81, 83
David, Jaques-Louis, 52
de Gruchy, John W., 32, 68, 87
democratic, 3, 22, 33, 49, 78
Devereux, Mary, 1, 87
dictatorship; dictator, 3, 33, 35, 39, 43, 45, 56, 73, 82; 78
Dietrich, Walter, 28, 87
distance, 3, 5, 16, 17, 23, 29, 34, 48, 49, 69, 70, 72, 85, 86
Dube, Musa W., 23, 88
Ebach, Jürgen, 42, 88
Elger, Dietmar, 35, 38, 39, 44, 47, 48, 88
Emcke, Carolin, 76
Enslin, Gudrun, 45, 47, 48, 49, 55, 82, 88
Enwezor, Okwui, 23, 88
epoch; epochal 39, 73; 22, 23, 24
Erbele-Küster, Dorothea, 29, 88
ethics, 1, 2, 5, 13, 31
Eufinger, Heinrich, 38
euthanasia, 35, 37, 38
evil, 1, 2, 5, 10, 13, 16, 29, 41, 73, 75, 82, 87
Fanon, Frantz, 69, 77, 88
fascism; fascist, 76; 33, 45
forgiveness, 3, 31, 32, 64, 75, 76, 77, 79, 81, 92
Freire, Paulo, 2, 78, 91
Frettlöh, Magdalena, 42, 88
Freud, Sigmund, 77

Friedel, Helmut, 44, 88
Fukuyama, Francis, 24, 88
fundamentalism; fundamentalist, 13, 16, 28; 9, 82
Gates, Bill, 7
generative themes, 2, 28, 85, 86
Germany, 2, 3, 7, 31, 32, 33, 35, 48, 79, 85, 90, 93
Global South, 23, 26, 67, 86
globalization, 3, 9, 23, 24, 26, 86
God, 1, 2, 3, 4, 5, 7, 8, 9, 11, 22, 24, 25, 26, 27, 28, 29, 31, 32, 56, 76, 79, 80, 81, 82, 83, 85, 88, 89
Gollwitzer, Helmut, 45, 46
Grabowski, Klaus H., 23, 88
grace, 4, 29, 31, 32, 33, 56, 79, 80, 82
Graf, Friedrich Wilhelm, 27, 88
Graham, Bob, 72, 88
Gregory, James, 72, 88
Griffith, Lee, 28, 88
Ground Zero, 5, 6, 19, 22, 91
guilt, 3, 31, 32, 35, 40, 42, 56, 73, 76, 81, 93
Habermas, Jürgen, 76
Hardt, Michael, 6, 88
Hermann, Jörg, 45, 46, 88
hermeneutics; hermeneutical, 85; 86
Heyde, Werner, 35, 37, 38
Hielscher, Martin, 40, 90
Hillegaart, Heinz, 75
Hillegaart, Viveka, 75, 76
Hirschler, Horst, 28, 88
Holbein, Franz, 53
Holderberg, Angelika, 76, 88
Hong, Song-Dam, 3, 32, 34, 35, 41, 43, 51, 53, 54, 56, 57, 58, 59, 60, 69, 62, 63, 64, 72, 74, 75, 78, 88
Horn, Rebekka, 2, 11, 12, 89
horror; horrible, 1, 2, 20, 32, 44, 48, 73, 74, 75; 33, 39, 40, 44
Huber, Wolfgang, 46, 75, 79, 89
human rights, 7, 69
Huntington, Samuel P., 11, 24, 89, 91
Hwang, Sok-Yong, 3, 32, 41, 56, 65, 74, 75, 89
icon, 10, 24, 37, 67, 68
iconoclasm, 12

identity, 2, 16, 23, 33, 38, 74
idolatry, 28
image (prohibition of), 2, 3, 4, 5, 6, 7, 10, 12, 18, 19, 22, 24, 27, 28, 29, 33, 67, 68
imperialism, 3, 39, 45, 67, 91
Islam; Muslim, 8, 9, 10, 16, 25, 28, 29, 89, 90, 91; 2, 3, 8, 11, 13, 16, 25, 27, 28, 91
Jaar, Alfredo, 2, 7, 8
Jeanrond, Werner G., 27, 89
Jewish; Judaism, 2, 11, 27, 28, 29, 44, 91
Jung, Andreas, 34, 87
justice, 4, 25, 29, 32, 56, 68, 72, 77, 80, 81, 82, 87
Kermani, Navid, 25, 89
Kim, Dae-Jung, 33, 41
Kim, Chi-Ha, 59, 78
Kim, Jong-Un, 33
Kim, Sung-Soo, 51, 89
Kim, Young-II, 33
Klar, Christian, 75, 79
Kraushaar, Wolfgang, 3, 45, 88, 89, 92
Krog, Antjie, 3, 31, 65, 72, 73, 74, 75, 77, 89
Küenzlen, Gottfried, 9, 89
Kurras, Karl-Heinz, 67
Küster, Volker, 2, 26, 28, 29, 86, 89
Kwangju, 3, 34, 43, 49, 51, 52, 53, 56, 57, 65
Kwok, Pui-Lan, 6, 91
Landau, Sigalit, 16
Lande, Aasulf, 27, 89
Lash, Scott, 24, 91
Lee, Myung-Bak, 33
Levinson, Jerrold, 1, 87
Lim, Chung-Hee, 34, 87
Link, Christian, 28, 29, 87
literature, 1, 2, 3, 39
Loach, Ken, 23
Lutterbach, Hubertus, 9, 89, 90
Mackert, Gabriele, 6, 90
Magesa, Laurenti, 23
Maluleke, Tinyiko, 23, 90
Mandela, Nelson, 7, 68, 72, 88, 90, 91
Manemann, Jürgen, 9, 89, 90

Index 97

Margalit, Avishai, 9, 87
Martig, Charles, 11, 90
massacre, 3, 34, 41, 43, 51, 56
media, 1, 6, 7, 10, 19, 22, 46, 64, 70, 72, 76
Meinhof, Ulrike, 47, 48, 49, 53, 82, 88
memoria passionis, 11, 26, 29, 73, 79, 83, 90
memory, 2, 5, 6, 12, 19, 22, 24, 26, 37, 44, 65, 72, 73, 74, 79
mercy, 3, 31, 32, 72, 74, 78, 79, 80
Mernissi, Fatima, 27
Metz, Johann Baptist, 11, 22, 26, 29, 56, 73, 79, 83, 90
military, 3, 6, 7, 13, 22, 25, 33, 43, 56, 78, 82
Minh, Ho Chi, 10
Minjung, 26, 34, 41, 51, 82, 85, 87, 89, 90, 93
Mohnhaupt, Brigitte, 75
Moltmann, Jürgen, 22, 27, 28, 83, 90
Moore, Michael, 10, 90
morally; morality, 10 ;13
Morrison, Toni, 3, 11, 22, 91
Müller, Harald, 9, 11, 91
Nazi, 35, 37, 38, 39, 44, 45, 46, 48, 67, 76
Negri, Antonio, 6, 88
neo-liberal, 3, 24, 28
Neshat, Shirin, 3, 15, 16, 17, 91
Niemöller, Martin, 46
Nirumand, Bahamãn, 67, 91
Ohnesorg, Benno, 40, 45, 67
oppression; oppressor, 2, 9, 23, 25, 85, 86; 69, 77
Pachlevi, Mohammed Reza, 67
painting, 3, 18, 34, 35, 37, 39, 41, 44, 47, 48, 49, 52, 55, 56, 58, 59, 60, 64, 65, 66, 69, 85, 92
Panikkar, Raimundo, 27, 91
Park, Chung-Hee, 43, 78
Park, Geun-Hye, 33, 78
passion, 3, 26, 49, 56, 74, 89
Penn, Sean, 23
perpetrator, 3, 4, 33, 35, 56, 68, 69, 72, 73, 74, 75, 76, 80, 81, 82, 83
Plaskow, Judith, 27

policy; political, 9, 23, 45; 2, 7, 13, 24, 26, 28, 31, 32, 34, 35, 39, 41, 46, 47, 64, 65, 69, 71, 78, 83, 86, 93
Ponto, Corinna, 80
Ponto, Jürgen, 46
poor, 9, 26, 27, 28, 34, 41, 80, 81, 85
Proll, Thorwald, 45
Putin, Wladimir, 23, 34
Raad, Walid, 3, 13, 14, 15, 16
Rahner, Karl, 27
Ramaphosa, Cyril, 68
Raspe, Jan-Carl, 55
reconciliation; reconcile, 2, 31, 32, 33, 42, 56, 64, 69, 76, 78, 86, 87, 92, 93; 4, 65
religion, 1, 2, 8, 9, 10, 11, 15, 25, 27, 28, 29, 51, 82, 85, 88, 89, 90
reparation, 3, 68, 69, 77, 79
repentance, 3, 64, 74, 75, 76, 77, 78, 80, 81
requiem, 40, 67
Rho, Tae-Woo, 43
Richter, Gerhard, 3, 17, 18, 19, 31, 35, 36, 37, 38, 39, 41, 44, 46, 47, 48, 49, 50, 52, 54, 55, 56, 74, 88, 89, 91, 92
Riefenstahl, Leni, 1, 16, 87
Robben Island, 7, 72
Robertson, Roland, 24, 91
Rosiny, Stephan, 25, 91
Roy, Arundhati, 3, 10
Russel, Letty M., 27, 91
Sahi, Joti, 12, 91
Said, Edward W., 3, 91
Sampson, Anthony, 72, 91
Satre, Jean Paul, 46, 92
Schleyer, Hans Martin, 45
Schneede, Uwe, 37, 89
Schnibben, Cordt, 11, 87
Schreiber, Jürgen, 38, 91
Schreiter, Robert J., 3, 24, 28, 90, 91
Schröder, Gerhard, 2
Schwarzenegger, Arnold, 11
Schwarzkogler, Rudolf, 16
Schwerfel, Heinz Peter, 5, 91
secularization; secular, 1; 2, 32, 80, 85, 86

Seel, Martin, 1, 91
self-reconciliation, 64, 77
September 11; 9/11, 2, 5, 9, 11, 13, 18, 23, 25, 28, 87, 88, 89, 90, 91, 92; 2, 3, 5, 6, 7, 10, 11, 12, 13, 17, 19, 20, 21, 22, 23, 24, 25, 47, 74, 86, 90
Shiva, Vandana, 27
Siemens, Anne, 45, 75, 76, 80, 91
Silverman, Kaja, 47
Simon, Benjamin, 64, 92
sin, 81
Small, Adam, 2, 31, 86
Sobrino, Jon, 81
Söhnlein, Horst, 45
Sontag, Susan, 1, 3, 9, 10, 13, 47, 91
Soong, Won-Cha, 51
soteriological circle, 56, 73, 79
South Africa, 2, 3, 23, 31, 32, 68, 69, 70, 74, 75, 78, 79, 82, 85, 92, 93
South Korea, 2, 3, 31, 33, 34, 49, 65, 67, 78, 79, 82, 92
Stockhausen, Karl Heinz, 2, 5, 13, 47, 86
Stopforth, Paul, 3, 71, 70
Storr, Robert, 18, 44, 47, 49, 52, 56, 92
story; stories, 41, 49, 56, 65, 72, 74, 80, 81; 2, 25, 68, 77, 85, 86
suffering, 2, 3, 26, 33, 40, 44, 56, 66, 68, 73, 75, 77, 82, 85
Sugirtharajah, R.S., 3, 92
Sundermeier, Theo, 65, 92
symbol, 3, 7, 10, 12, 13, 24, 56, 58, 61, 64, 79
Tamez, Elsa, 81, 92
Tanovic, Danis, 23
terrorism; terrorists, 2, 3, 6, 12, 13, 16, 28, 46, 49, 88, 91; 5, 6, 7, 9, 10, 12, 13, 22, 25, 45, 46, 47, 49, 74, 75, 80
theodicy, 11, 82
Timm, Uwe, 3, 32, 39, 40, 41, 67, 68, 74, 75, 92

torture; torturer, 7, 34, 58, 59, 60, 65; 64, 69, 72, 77
transformation, 3, 31, 68, 73, 87
trauma; traumatic, 26, 43, 64, 73; 32, 43
Trible, Phyllis, 27, 29, 91, 92
Trump, Donald, 34
Tutu, Desmond, 76, 77, 78, 79, 92
ugly, 73
unscathedness, 3, 5, 17, 29, 86
van der Schoot, Albert, 5
Verwoerd, Wilhelm, 69, 92
victim, 3, 4, 11, 19, 20, 21, 22, 23, 33, 39, 40, 42, 45, 46, 49, 56, 59, 65, 67, 68, 69, 73, 74, 75, 76, 77, 79, 80, 81, 82, 83
Villa-Vincencio, Charles, 69, 92
violence, 2, 5, 16, 26, 45, 67, 81, 86
Virilio, Paul, 12, 92
vision, 3, 5, 10, 16, 17, 29
visual arts, 1
von Aretin, Felicitas, 23, 88, 92
von Mirbach, Andreas, 76
von Mirbach, Christa, 76
von Mirbach, Clais, 76
vulnerability, 3, 13, 48
Wadud, Amina, 27
Walker, Peter, 19, 20, 21
Walter, Dietrich, 28, 87
Walther, Rudolf, 3, 92
Wannenmacher, Bernd, 23, 88, 92
war, 2, 3, 5, 6, 7, 10, 11, 13, 15, 21, 23, 24, 26, 28, 29, 33, 35, 37, 38, 39, 40, 41, 42, 43, 45, 46, 49, 73, 88, 91
Weems, Benjamin B., 51, 92
Weiermair, Peter, 16, 92
Welten, Ruud, 46, 92
Wickert, Ulrich, 10
Williamson, Sue, 3, 69, 70, 72, 74, 75, 92
World Trade Center, 12, 19, 22
writer, 2, 10, 31, 32, 39, 40, 41, 67, 72
Zijlstra, Onno, 1

www.ingramcontent.com/pod-product-compliance
Lightning Source LLC
Chambersburg PA
CBHW061245230426
43662CB00020B/2432